Chasing Rainbows

Exploring Gender Fluid Parenting Practices

Chasing Rainbows

Exploring Gender Fluid
Parenting Practices

Edited by

Fiona Joy Green and May Friedman

DEMETER

DEMETER PRESS

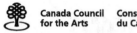

Canada Council   Conseil des Arts
for the Arts   du Canada

The publisher gratefully acknowledges the support of the Canada Council for the Arts for its publishing program.

Demeter Press logo based on the sculpture "Demeter" by Maria-Luise Bodirsky <www.keramik-atelier.bodirsky.de>

Printed and Bound in Canada

Library and Archives Canada Cataloguing in Publication

        Chasing rainbows: exploring gender fluid parenting practices / edited by Fiona Joy Green and May Friedman.

Includes bibliographical references.
ISBN 978-1-927335-18-5

Cataloguing data available from Library and Archives Canada.

Demeter Press
140 Holland Street West
P. O. Box 13022
Bradford, ON L3Z 2Y5
Tel: (905) 775-9089
Email: info@demeterpress.org
Website: www.demeterpress.org

*To the parents and children who are bravely
and courageously living their lives by honouring
and supporting fluid gender expression*

Table of Contents

Acknowledgements

This book has been a labour of love inspired by the many parents, children and families around us who experiment with gender and self-expression in radical and innovative ways. In particular, this book began from many conversations provoked by the brave words and actions of Kathy Witterick and David Stocker; we are in awe of their strength and so very grateful for their hard work. Like-wise, the contributors to this volume have courageously pushed forward in both personal and scholarly contexts to uphold the need for gender fluidity.

Without the support of Demeter Press, there would be no venue for us to explore these topics; to Demeter and especially our editorial matriarch, Andrea O'Reilly, we give great thanks. May would like to especially thank her family of origin, her family of now, and her families of choice for constantly participating in stimulating and complicated conversations. Fiona is particularly thankful for her partner, son, students and colleagues who courageously explore gender self-expression and persistently examine theories of gender identity. She is also most grateful for her siblings' never wavering belief in and support of her parenting practices.

Introduction

MAY FRIEDMAN AND FIONA JOY GREEN

S OME DAYS IT FEELS LIKE the present moment has never been
more ripe for exploration of gender fluidity. Thomas Beatie,
the pregnant man (Beatie), books such as Kate Bornstein and
Bear Bergman's collection *Gender Outlaws: The Next Generation*
and myriad blogs exploring gender fluidity and experimentation,[1]
suggest that gender may be increasingly viewed more effectively as
a continuum rather than a binary. This is hardly news to feminists
who have delved into Judith Butler and Bornstein; to activists who
have pushed for the right to transition; for many people who have
welcomed the slippery play of gender instead of its rigid binary
outlines. Yet the backlash to every effort to explore gender in creative and non-normative ways suggests that, in the midst of these
exciting fissures and pressure points, gender continues to serve as
a stolid and uncompromising arbiter of human behaviour, and
that efforts to transgress strict gender binary are incredibly risky.
Chasing Rainbows: Exploring Gender Fluid Parenting Practices
seeks to explore the tensions between both an increasing exploration of gender and the turgid intransigence of the expectations
of parents to raise blue boys and pink girls to become good (and
obedient) men and women.

Feminist parents may attempt to resist gender binaries; they
may submit to them while attempting to foster critical dialogue;
they may struggle with the display of their own femininity and
masculinity or, for some, its perceived lack. For some parents a
dialogue about gender normativity may be inspired by gender-diverse behaviour on the part of their own children, while others

may parent children who happily submit to the mainstream and query the need for gender questioning. This collection casts a lens on the messy and convoluted ways that querying parents approach parenting their children in gender aware and gender fluid ways. Scholars, activists and community members have participated in a conversation about the challenges of exploring and maintaining an awareness of gender while parenting in a highly gender normative world.

Tey Meadow suggests that, "Over the last century, there has been a proliferation within biomedicine, psychiatry and popular culture, of the ways in which we can 'know' gender; and as a result, individuals are called upon to understand and communicate our gender in ever increasing detail" (727). More colloquially, Kate Bornstein professes herself "thrilled" with the evolution of gender play, "awed by the heights from which this gen[eration] of gender outlaws has leapt off into their unexplored spaces. People today are STARTING from further than I go to when I'd finished writing *Gender Outlaws...*" (Bornstein and Bergman 11). Many of the contributors of this book are living and parenting in ways that are transgressive and risky, and are exploring new fractures in the gender bulwark, responding to cultural shifts about gender fluidity, gender non-conformity and gender awareness. Lest we become self-congratulatory, however, the backlash continues and can be seen in the event which inspired this collection: the birth of a baby named Storm.

STORM

This collection aims to explore some of the ways that parents are choosing to respect gender fluidity through their personal expression and/or the ways parents are raising children to honour their children's fluid expression of gender. The book was highly influenced by the brave actions of a Canadian family in 2011 that spurred international publicity, interest and debate.

The decision of Toronto parents Kathy Witterick and David Stocker to keep the sex of their youngest child, Storm, a private matter among themselves, their other children, and a family friend and the midwives present at Storm's birth, was made partly in response to watching their first two children, then five-year-old Jazz and three-year-old Kio, as well as adults in their lives, express their gender in ways that are considered by most to be unconventional. Witterick and Stocker believe children are capable of making their own decisions and want to reduce the constraints of what's expected to be male or female placed on their children. Before becoming parents, Witterick was engaged in feminist activism and worked as the provincial and then national lead trainer on healthy child development for a research-based child advocacy group, before delivering violence and abuse prevention workshops in high schools around Ontario for years with the Canadian Red Cross. Stocker worked at an alternative school based on anti-oppression and social justice work with youth for over a decade and is the author of an award-winning book linking the teaching of mathematics with social justice issues. Drawing on these experiences, doing some further research, and speaking with Jazz and Kio, they chose to keep Storm's sex private among their family. They believe the best way to nurture, honour and respect Storm's development is to allow Storm the time and space to explore and feel comfortable with her/his gender identity and expression. They are sure that Storm will let folks know when the time is right.

The media frenzy that followed the publication of their story in *The Toronto Star* on May 21, 2011 was overwhelming. Witterick and Stocker, along with their three children, were thrust into the public eye through reports on television, radio, Twitter and blogs. Their photographs, which were first published in the original article, quickly appeared online, on TV, and in print. Curious journalists phoned, emailed, and even turned up on their doorstep wanting to interview the family. Storm's parents declined requests from NBC, *National Geographic*, *60 Minutes Australia*, Anderson Cooper, *Dr. Phil*, and the Oprah Winfrey Network (Poisson). Strangers delivered angry letters to their door and shouted their incensed predictions of Storm's gender as they drove by in cars. "Experts" and strangers alike weighed in online, in the press, on talk shows, and on news reports with their often-uninformed opinions about Witterick and Stocker's decision, parenting abilities, and potential negative consequences for Storm, Kio and Jazz.

People who accept or believe in strict gender boundaries and binaries have difficulty understanding an affirmative approach to child rearing that fosters a space where children are free to explore and experiment with their gender. Encouraging children's self-assertion of who they are is central to raising gender creative children, yet it's threatening to those who are fearful of diverse gender expression; sadly, gender-based bullying is often a result of strict gender expectations (Desjardins).

Yet, alongside the negative and vitriolic responses, the family received many affirming messages from people who, despite the challenges, are successfully living their lives in ways that provide opportunities for themselves and their children to live in ways that more accurately reflect their gender identities and, subsequently, contest established gender roles. They also found a community made up of researchers, authors, activists, and parents who, like them, are thinking carefully about the kind of communities to which they would like to belong and in which they would like to raise their children.

WHY GENDER FLUID?

In helping children express their gender in ways that feel comfortable to them and which don't conform to strict socially prescribed gender roles and expressions, many parents attempt to alter the boundaries and binaries of gender. They assist their children's gender creativity by affording their kids multiple opportunities to develop and practice their self-expression. With love and support within and outside their homes, families and communities, these children explore their gender creativity through clothing choices, play, activities, toys, book, films, and language. They also join a community of folks around them who model various ways of being gendered in the world. Regardless of gender identity, all children explore what makes them feel both comfortable and uncomfortable in relation to their gender. Through trial and error, they learn what makes them feel good about themselves. All kids are more able to practice self-determination in environments that are supportive, validating and affirming; parents are likewise able to explore and transgress gender in considerate and supported communities. Gender fluid parenting approaches assist in creating such spaces. We hope that *Chasing Rainbows* both documents the hard work of creating thoughtful and gender critical families and communities and also, as a collection, supports the families and communities around us.

Chasing Rainbows hopes to positively contribute to the conversation about the necessity for approaching parenting in ways that nourish, support, and protect children and families as they learn who they are and how they want to express their gendered selves. We hope that this collection positions gender fluid parenting practices as deeply healthy and profoundly normal and simultaneously part of an exhilarating, often terrifying and deeply radical cultural shift.

WHERE WE BEGIN

As with all political fights, we come to this discussion and collection from varied positionings. We want to share our points of entry to this topic, our own experiences of the enmeshed "personal" and "political."

Fiona:

While I've only recently come to the language of gender fluidity, I've been familiar with the need for, and have engaged in, the practice of honouring and nourishing the self-determined gender expression of children, youth and adults since birthing my son twenty-five years ago. Gender fluid parenting has been an embodied experience that has grown organically through my relationship with my curious and self-assured son who, since preschool, has been consciously exploring and practicing his gender. While we certainly continue to face challenges, particularly those presented by other people's narrow thinking and fear that are often informed by patriarchy and other intersecting systems of power and domination, the journey has mostly been positive.

A quarter of a century ago our little family of three was rather isolated in our experience and was considered a strange anomaly by many family members, friends and acquaintances. Yet today, we are part of an emergent community of people who are engaged in shifting the consciousness around autonomy and self-identity:

a community of folks who are interested in understanding the complexities of and supporting the rich diversity of being human. This growing community is made up of people in various personal and public circles that are both locally based and increasingly part of an extended series of geographically global friendships and affiliations through the Internet, social media and other networks.

I see the contributors of this anthology as part of this growing and powerful movement that's committed to sharing experiential and scholarly knowledge. It's my belief that as people engage in the politics of visibility as public intellectuals, the void of knowledge about gender fluidity will begin to be replaced by a matrix of resourceful, respectful and multifaceted perspectives. My hope is that *Chasing Rainbows* provokes discussion around the complexities and politics of gender, families and parenting, in addition to offering a variety of perspectives and strategies that are helpful to creating positive social change for all.

May:

My third child was born eleven days before Storm and two weeks after I completed my doctorate in women's studies. When Storm's story hit the world stage, I found myself expected to comment in my twin roles as feminist academic and parent of a Storm-sized baby. Suddenly, at a haircut, a drop in, a family bar mitzvah, I was meant to articulately express my opinion on this unique parenting decision, usually while breastfeeding and/or parenting my older children. In the fog of my own challenges with transition, I struggled to convey my admiration for Kathy and David, my outrage at the horrifying ways they were being portrayed, and my grief at the primacy of gender being made so evident. Yet my own parenting choices were constantly seen as trumping any expertise or opinion I might put forth—my own children's evident genders somehow seemed to allow those around me to make peace with my feminist principles because they weren't pushing "too far."

I want to push too far. If there is a guiding principle of my life and my scholarship, it's a commitment to trouble-making, to exploring the fuzzy edges and exploding the concretization of so-called truths. While I have made different choices from those made in Storm's family, I would not hesitate to ally myself with them; I also see a diversity of tactics as essential to any revolution. Two years out from that post-partum fog, I am still in awe at the courage and strength of Storm's parents; I am still upset, though not surprised, at the extent to which the backlash against them conveys the rigidity of the gender systems which hold us in their grip.

For me, this collection is an examination of the revolution which is brewing in parenting practice, and an exploration of that diversity of tactics. This book has allowed me to consider what methods we may use to push back against gender as a principle organizing system and to convey, perhaps more articulately than I was able to in the midst of my sleep-deprived newborn haze, my commitment to interrupting gender in my life and my parenting.

THEMES

While we have our own scholarly and emotional points of entry to thinking about gender fluid parenting, the contributors to this collection likewise present a range of personal and academic orientations to the topic. The chapters in *Chasing Rainbows* reflect a number of key themes that may be situated within a broader literature around gender, identity and subjectivity.

Praxis

One of the central themes found in this collection is praxis—the cyclical process of consciously putting one's ideas and understandings into practice, while also reflecting upon the influence that those embodied actions may have on one's beliefs. From an Aristotelian perspective, the purpose of praxis is to enact one's conscious knowledge and practical wisdom with the ethical and political intention of living well (Bernstein xiv). In the case of gender fluidity, people who hold alternative, more complex and diverse understandings of gender than the narrow, socially prescribed cisgender binary,[2] often learn to develop and trust their own experiential knowledge and practical wisdom in their efforts to live in ways that reflect their genuine selves. They do so, however, in a world that does not respect nor reflect their embodiment of gender, or support their vision and practice of gender diversity. These beliefs are skillfully articulated in the chapters of this collection, perhaps most touch-ingly in the numerous autoethnographic offerings that take up, in detail, the harrowing work of translating strong ideological beliefs into the messy world of parenting.

By engaging in a praxis that's based on a belief that bifurcated sex/gender categories and positions do not speak to their reality, gender non-conforming folks and their allies complicate the truth about gender (Butler). This act of complicating the truth about gender often requires using the strategies of resistance and rework-ing (Katz 242; Schneider), as well as finding and creating places that, while not always protected or safe, offer opportunities where people's identities can emerge through performance, modeling, and exposure to multiple gender expressions (Gregson and Rose; Schneider). These strategies and spaces also offer various occasions for people to develop and trust their own experiential knowledge (Williams), and to create networks and communities of supportive allies. These traits are shown amply in many chapters. While the terminology may change (for example, an examination of feminist parenting) and the specific circumstances may vary (for example, a study of parents of gender non-conforming children), the theme of praxis holds true across these differences.

Reworking and Resistance

According to Cindi Katz and Sandra Schneider, reworking is the process whereby people, after acknowledging a problem, consciously implement practices that change the conditions of the everyday in hopes of facilitating a more agreeable life and a collec-tive capacity for broader change. Through the act of reworking, individuals learn to become "political subjects and social actors" (Katz 205). They also develop an "oppositional consciousness" (Katz 251; Hossler 106), which interrogates, troubles, contests and rejects restrictive and oppressive social relations that produce and maintain ideologies and practices such as gendernormativity, heteronormativity and cisnormativity.[3] Oppositional conscious-ness is "consciously non-normative" and, within the context of promoting gender fluidity, intentionally aims to maintain a critical distance from gender binary and cisgender norms (Schneider, this volume).

8

In addition to the dynamic process of reworking and the intentional practice of oppositional consciousness, gender self-determination and advocacy for gender diversity require active resistance to dualistic and dichotomous gender identities, roles, stereotypes, ideals, expectations and norms (Jessica). Such mindful and attentive resistance is found and enacted in multiple ways and in various locations, both in the world and in this book.

For example, folks engage in strategies that include, but are not limited to, participating in discursive and behavioural practices with the aim to help expand notions of gender, preserve gender options, negotiate new identities, and offer multiple role models (Moore and Moore). Other strategies may include critically reviewing language, discourse, messaging, and imagery found in books, films, advertising, mainstream and alternative media and popular culture, as well as in toys, clothes, games and personal interactions. Challenging the attitudes and behaviours of others through various means is also an example of resistance.

Whatever they entail, acts of resistance can take place in small, intimate settings through private conversations in person, over the phone and on line, as well as in larger and more public activities such as parades, performances, camps or media events. All of these approaches illustrate the ways in which folks think about and willfully respond to resisting gender normative scripts and expectations.

Community

Central to the advancement of praxis, reworking and resistance are communities and networks that are based on trust. Trust with individuals and communities develops over time, and is based on the personal relationships and connections among those who are living in, and engaging with, the community. Networks and communities often develop in ad hoc ways through families, friends, and allies who may be variously connected to individuals, groups and/or collectives that are in local areas, or are more geographically dispersed. As some chapters in this book convey, however, the overlap of many different communities of alliance may sometimes result in contradictory positions or uncomfortable negotiations.

Within these communities, individuals and families often find allies who share their experiences and perspectives and who are frequently able to offer understanding, support and strategies. It is here that they may learn about the hidden histories of discrimination and oppression (Schneider, this volume), the ways in which most people internalize the damaging messages of such histories (Bishop), and the valuable lessons of how to deconstruct such ideologies and practices (Pharr).

These communities can create liminoid spaces, where the "time and space betwixt and between one context of meaning and action and another" may offer opportunities for people to discover, fashion, and celebrate subversive gender exploration and expression (Turner 54). Such spaces may present "a variant model for thought and action [that can] be accepted or rejected after careful consideration," as well as a number of "subjective" possibilities for observing and engaging in gender fluidity (Turner 54).

To be successful, these liminoid spaces, and the people in them, must feel trustworthy. They must also offer what bell hooks calls "homeplace"—a network of "spaces, places, people, events, histories, practices, and care that offer respite and help people recuperate from a hostile normative world" (Schneider 115), this volume). As many contributors in this collection demonstrate, parents often intentionally look to community with the aim to create safer places for their children.[4] Within a community of allies, gender variant individuals may find homeplace spaces that can present occasions to engage with others in ways that undermine gender roles, norms, expectations and stereotypes, in addition to providing opportunities where they can craft themselves in ways that feel right and authentic.

Fear, Risk and Authenticity

The chapters in this collection suggest that there is a strong relationship between thinking about gender and thinking about risk. Authors make clear that they are aware of the potential impact of making non-normative choices and allowing young people to be subjected to ridicule. As a result many authors document complicated negotiations between the public and private spheres. Other chapters look at the decisions of feminist parents and parents of gender diverse children to negotiate on behalf of their children and with their children with safety foremost among their considerations. At the same time, this collection solidifies an important perspective on risk and safety: the authors in this book make it very clear that there is a grave risk of inaction, of entrenching normative gender roles to avoid short term pain at the risk of long term physical, social and spiritual health. As a result, the book suggests that negotiations of gender fluidity in parenting can sometimes feel like a minefield.

While the chapters make clear that the reality of gender does not fit into two neat boxes, for parents and children alike, the specific experiences of parents show the tension between keeping children safe and encouraging them to push the envelope. The overall conclusion over and over, of course, is that pushing the envelope, as children, parents, and societies is the only way to keep us, individually and collectively, safe and healthy. It is easy to state this glibly, but the authors of this book make it clear that navigating these choices is not for the faint of heart, that it requires endless grappling and negotiation between the utopia we aspire toward and the complicated and often dangerous world which we inhabit.

While many parents discussed in this book are concerned with their children's physical safety and the potential backlash at nonconformity, there emerges a related theme of authenticity and critical dialogue. Contributors consider the ways that gender fluid parenting may be part of a continuum of critical and engaged parenting choices. This is true across gender but also in consideration of cultures, abilities, classes and sexuality—it is not by accident that the contributors to this book do not succeed in describing gender in isolation. The conclusion drawn by many contributions to this collection is that our overall goal for our children is to encourage authentic and actualized choices, and that the system of binary gender constrains all of us, adults and children, from doing so.

Identities vs. Practices

It can be tempting to discuss gender fluidity from the perspective of either identities—often in relation to transgendered or gender non-conforming children and grownups—or practices, as in the case of parents like Storm's. Interestingly, as with many other discourses, the element of choice is often presented in these dialogues in ways that seemingly vindicate certain subjectivities (poor dears, they can't help it) while villainizing certain practices (how dare they!). This "choice" is prevalent in discussions of gender fluid parenting where sympathetic media portrayals of gender non-conforming or transgendered young people are increasingly presented as within the realm of human potential. At the same time, as the backlash to Storm's discreetly private sex showed all too well, parents who take on practices who encourage gender non-conformity are seen as dangerous, misguided and abusive. The notion of gender non-conformity as a fixed identity, independent of "radical" parenting, follows other disagreeable tropes (such as the quest for the "gay gene" and the "fat gene," [LeBesco]) in suggesting that fluidity of human experience should not provoke negative reaction, regardless of how disagreeable it is. Instead, the increasing focus on non-normative subjectivities as both fixed and biological positions people in the blurry margins as victims, and suggests that we should love certain people with certain conditions despite their "afflictions."

At the same time, as this book aims to convey, gender non-conformity is not a foregone outcome of gender fluid parenting, any more than fixed gender binaries in parenting are insurance against gender play. The authors of this book make clear the oppressive implications of this approach by celebrating a gleeful and exuberant continuum of gendered behaviours and identities and by provoking us to consider the blurry margins as, in some respect, the spaces we all inhabit. We view gender as unfixed and independent of biology and in so doing, we are deeply committed to playing with gender as a central practice.

Chasing Rainbows suggests that in some cases, parents themselves "transition" in relation to their children's gender exploration, while in others, children may respond to their parents own non-normative identities and practices and grow up as safe, confident explorers. In either case, this collection suggests that fluid models of both identities and practices must be enthusiastically supported for the project of gender fluidity to gain traction.

THE CHAPTERS

The collection opens with Kathy Witterick's "Dancing in the Eye of the Storm," a grappling with the connections between her personal story and the broader politics of gender. Witterick critically exposes the machinations of gender conformity and the systems in whose interests it is undertaken by exploring the praxis between her personal experiences and the larger political landscape. Following Witterick's lead, in "Get Your Gender Binary Off My Childhood!: Towards a Movement for Children's Gender Self-Determination" Jane Ward provides a framework based on the insights of queer and feminist theory to assist adults in supporting the gender-creative potential of *all* children. She offers readers a set of practical guidelines based on her own queer parenting experiences to assist adults in fostering gender-self determination in children. The five guiding principles are predicated on actively cultivating children's familiarity with, and appreciation for, genderqueer identity and culture, and welcoming their engagement with gender signifiers without gender diagnosis.

In her autoethnographic piece Susan Goldberg presents an honest reckoning with the risks and benefits of supporting gender fluid play and dress. Her chapter, "The Boy in the Red Dress" focuses a critical lens on her own experiences of reinforcing gender exploration in her two-mom household. In exposing her own experiences, Goldberg forces us to confront the tensions between our own ideals and our ambivalence and concerns about children's safety.

Damien Riggs takes a macro look at similar themes to Goldberg in his model for mapping the unique experiences of men who undertake pregnancy in "Transgender Men's Self-Representations of Bearing Children Post-Transition." Using social scientific literature and public self-representations of transgender men who birth children, he demonstrates how these men negotiate with the role of father that excludes fathers as child bearers and argues that recognition of these men as fathers challenges the norms of historically defined pregnancy as the experiences of women only. Also looking at representation and gender non-conformity, in "Trapped in the Wrong Body and Life Uncharted: Anticipation and Identity within Narratives of Parenting Transgender/ Gender-Nonconforming Children," Jessica Ann Vooris explores the role of anticipation and identity within narratives found in television documentaries and blogs related to transgender and gender-creative children. She argues that while understanding identity categories as various, contextual and shifting is important when considering narratives about children's sexuality and gender, there is still a tendency for the stories of transgender and gay children to be more accepted than the narratives of children that are more ambiguous.

"We're Having a Stanley" is an autoethnographic account by j wallace of the journey towards parenthood undertaken together with his husband. Their "The Small Person Acquisition Project" focuses on the challenges and successes of providing their two-and-a-half year old child with gender choices and space for self-expression and self-exploration, as well as strategies for engaging with others in creating such gender fluid opportunities. May Friedman takes up similar challenges and strategies through the lenses of ethnicity and culture.

In "Between The Village and The Village People: Negotiating Community, Ethnicity and Safety in Gender Fluid Parenting," Friedman interrogates the challenges of honouring her heritage, culture and relationship with her family of origin, while also respecting her own understanding of feminism and her approach to raising her children in ways that encourage and support their gender development and expression. Her honest exploration reveals the complex ways in which children learn to develop and express their capacity to critically engage with and understand how gender intersects with the social systems of ethnicity, religion and class.

"Producing Homeplace: Strategic Sites and Liminoid Spaces for Gender-Diverse Children" documents a multi-year qualitative study of self-identified feminist parents in the Deep South and Appalachian regions of the United States. Sandra Schneider shows the complicated ways that these parents support their children's "gender health" by exploring liminoid spaces, spaces in which norms are viewed as provisional and shifting sites of engagement. These ideas are similarly explored by Jake Pyne in his chapter about a community based research project about trans parents in Toronto, focusing on the explicit parenting strengths which co-exist with the discrimination faced by many trans parents. Specifically, in "Complicating the Truth of Gender: Gender Literacy and the Possible Worlds of Trans Parenting," Pyne shows the ways that families which cannot easily take gender binary as a common-sense truth use this dynamic to ensure greater gender literacy, and more open gender choices for the children in their care.

In "Pink Butterflies and Blue Caterpillars," where Arwen Brenneman reflects on similar themes by sharing her experiences of trying to figure out what she means when, as new parents, she and her husband commit to raising "one of the good guys." She addresses some of the ways she has had to reflect upon her own understandings of and behaviour related to gender, the ways in which she has felt like a border guard protecting the space where her sons play with their self-expression, and the ways she continues to negotiate with her sons and others within her family and community to keep judgment from seeping in.

Sarah Sahagian considers the ways that heteronormative and gender confirming parenting models may hinder the capacity for interethnic cultural transmission. Sahagian's chapter, "I Wish I Knew How to Make Cabbage Rolls: An Explanation of Why The Future of Ethnicity Relies Upon Gender Fluidity" grapples with the twin influences of her Anglo-Saxon maternal cultural and her paternal Armenian heritage, reflecting on her complicated feelings of inauthenticity in both cultures. The chapter exposes the ways that a more nuanced and fluid approach to gendered parenting roles may contribute to a more honest reckoning of subjecthood across both gender and ethnicity. Elizabeth Rahilly's chapter "The Parental Transition: A Study of Parents of Gender Variant Children" explores the intense work undertaken by parents who support gender non-conforming and/or gender transitioning children. Rahilly considers the many transitions undertaken by parents themselves, including an increased politicization and critical awareness of the limitations of the binary gender system. As a result, the parents she interviewed now have ties to GLBT communities that would not necessarily exist otherwise. This may be the case for the final authors in this collection. Fiona Joy Green and Barry Edginton collaborate with their son, Liam Edginton-Green in a powerful piece which explores some of the implications of feminist and engaged gender fluid parenting into adulthood. "Our Fluid Family: Expression, Engagement and Feminism" portrays an intimate account of the differing starting points of these family members and the ways their commitment to exploration has led to shifting subjectivities for all three. The collection culminates with Liam Edginton-Green's honest reflections as an adult child raised with gender fluid values that have led to a robust and dynamic self-expression.

Chasing Rainbows: Exploring Gender Fluid Parenting Practices considers many ideas and themes and is the culmination of many deeply personal and emotional stories. We hope this book disrupts taken for granted "truths" and displays the bravery, grit, and agonizing self-reflection of many parents committed to gender fluidity. In the final analysis, however, the book is overwhelmingly about love, and about the grave constraints put on our capacities to love, ourselves and one other, authentically. In this spirit, we offer forth this collection with a spirit of love and hope it provokes continued conversations about how we can ensure a commitment to authenticity and freedom in our lives as parents and beyond.

[1]See for example: *Catching Our Rainbows; HE SPARKLES; It's A Bold Life; Labels Are For Jars; Lesbian Dad; Living An Examined Life; My Beautiful Little Boy; Pink Is For Boys; Raising My Rainbow; Raising Queer Kids; Sam's Stories; Sarah Hoffman.*
[2]Cisgender is a term developed by Hugh Crethar and Laurie Vargas to define an individual whose self-perception of their gender matches that of their sex (61).
[3]Cisnormativity is the body of social and cultural norms that view cisgender to be the normal gender orientation for people (Schilt and Westbrook).
[4]See Brenneman; Friedman; Green et al.; Goldberg; Pyne; Rahilly; Riggs; Sahagian; Schneider; wallace; Ward; and Witterick for examples within this collection.

WORKS CITED

Bishop, Anne. *Becoming an Ally: Breaking the Cycle of Oppression in People.* Black Point, NS: Fernwood, 2002. Print.

Beatie, Thomas. *Labour of Love: The Story of One Man's Extraordinary Pregnancy.* Berkeley, CA: Seal Press. 2008. Print.

Bernstein, Richard. "Preface." *Praxis and Action: Contemporary Philosophies of Human Activity.* Philadelphia: University of Pennsylvania Press, 1999. viii-xix. Print.

Bornstein, Kate and Bear Bergman, eds. *Gender Outlaws: The Next Generation.* Berkeley: Seal Press, 2010. Print.

Butler, Judith. *Undoing Gender.* New York: Routledge, 2004. Print.

Catching Our Rainbows. Web. Accessed February 12, 2013.

Crethar, Hugh. C. and Laurie A. Vargas. "Multicultural Intricacies in Professional Counseling." *The Counselor's Companion: What Every Beginning Counselor Needs to Know.* Eds. J. Gregoire and C. Jungers. Mahwah, NJ: Lawrence Erlbaum, 2007. 52-71. Print.

Desjardins, Cléa. "From Gender Identity Disorder to Gender Identity Creativity." EurekAlert.org. 11 October 2012. Web. Accessed January 29, 2013.

Gregson, Nicky and Gillian Rose. "Taking Butler Elsewhere: Performativities, Spatialities and Subjectivities." *Environment and Planning D: Society and Space* 18 (2000): 433-452. Print.

HE SPARKLES. Web. Accessed February 12, 2013.

hooks, bell. "Homeplace: A Site of Resistance." 1990. *Maternal Theory.* Ed. Andrea O'Reilly. Bradford, ON: Demeter Press, 2007. 382-390. Print.

Hossler, Peter. "Free Health Clinics, Resistance and the Entanglement of Christianity and Commodified Health Care Delivery" *Antipode* 44 (1) 2012: 98-121. Print.

It's A Bold Life. Design is Good Blogspot. Web. Accessed February 12, 2013.

It's Hard to Be Me: Parenting and Loving Our Gender Fluid Child. Gender Fluid Kid Blogspot. Web. Accessed February 12, 2013.

Jessica. *The Politics of Gender Self-Determination: More Interviews with Captive Genders Contributors.* July 26, 2011. Revolution by the Book: The AK Press Blog. Web. Accessed February 3, 2013.

Katz, Cindi. *Growing up Global: Economic Restructuring and Children's Everyday Lives*. Minneapolis: University of Minnesota Press, 2004. Print.

Labels Are For Jars. Web. Accessed February 12, 2013

LeBesco, Kathleen. "Quest For a Cause: The Fat Gene, the Gay Gene and the New Eugenics." *The Fat Studies Reader*. Eds. Esther Rothblum and Sandra Solovay. New York: New York University Press, 2009. 65-75. Print.

Lesbian Dad. Web. Accessed February 12, 2013.

Life Uncharted. Web. Accessed February 12, 2013.

Living An Examined Life. Web. Accessed February 12, 2013.

Meadow, Tey. "'Deep Down Where the Music Plays': How Parents Account for Childhood Gender Variance." *Sexualities* 14.6 (2011): 725-747. Print.

Moore, Tom and Scott Moore. *My Pregnant Dad 20/20 Interview*. August 25, 2011. Print.

My Beautiful Little Boy. Web. Accessed February 12, 2013.

Pharr, Suzanne. *Homophobia: A Weapon of Sexism*. Berkeley, CA: Chardon Press, 2002. Print.

Pink is For Boys. Web. Accessed February 12, 2013.

Poisson, Jayme. "The 'Genderless Baby' Who Caused a Storm of Controversy in 2011." 26 December 2011. *The Toronto Star* Web. Accessed January 27, 2013.

Raising My Rainbow. Web. Accessed February 12, 2013.

Raising Queer Kids. Web. Accessed February 12, 2013.

Sam's Stories. Web. Accessed February 12, 2013. Schilt, Kristen and Larel Westbrook. 2009. "Doing Gender, Doing Heteronormativity: 'Gender Normals,' Transgender People, and the Social Maintenance of Heterosexuality." *Gender & Society* 23 (4) (2009): 440-464. Print.

Schneider, Sandra. "Feminist Parents' Strategic Use of Liminoid Experiences to Produce Sites of Empowerment for Young Gender-Diverse Children." *Chasing Rainbows: Exploring Gender Fluid Parenting Practices*. Eds. Fiona Joy Green and May Friedman. Bradford, ON: Demeter Press. 201. 111-126. Print.

Turner, Victor. "Acting in Everyday Life and Everyday Life in Acting." *Humanities in Review. Volume 1*. Eds. Ronald Dworkin, Karl Miller, and Richard Sennett. London: The New York

Institute for the Humanities/Cambridge University Press, 1982. 83-105. Print.

Williams, Patricia J. *The Alchemy of Race and Rights: Diary of a Law Professor*. Cambridge: Harvard, 1992. Print.

David Stocker, "Zenith," 2013, acrylic on canvas, 16" x 28". Toronto, Ontario.

1.
Dancing in the Eye of the Storm

The Gift of Gender Diversity to Our Family

KATHY WITTERICK

THE ARTWORK ON THE OPPOSITE PAGE is painted by my partner, David.[1] It shows our child, Jazz, at the top of an up-swing, on the cusp of an exhilarating descent. It's a moment with potential. It shines with Jazz's confidence to meet it with joyfulness. Over coffee, I asked Princeton academic Tey Meadow which commonalities united the gender non-conforming children in her study. I understood when she said, "Courage." Our family's revolution is personal. But go ahead, take a look. It *is* personal. But, I also realize, it's not.

BACKGROUND

Near winter solstice this year, Jazz wanted to discuss a pronoun change. It was nearly two years since Storm first saw light. Storm arrived as a sibling to five-year-old Jazz and three-year-old Kio, two strong-minded kids who paved the way for unconventional choices in our family. Our kids taught us that gender is about identity and it takes time to be expressed and we had noticed that few adults nurture gender exploration beyond the status quo. We decided not to announce what we didn't know. Storm's unambiguous physiology was a named fact in the family but we didn't offer sex disclosure publicly or succumb to assigning gender on balloons or announcement cards. When quizzed by strangers, the kids responded offhandedly, "Someday, Storm'll tell you." A few weeks after David returned to work from parental leave, a reporter approached us. Galvanized by the unanticipated benefits to our

21

family of our choice, we granted a short interview one sunny spring morning. On May 21st, Storm's four-month-old smile brightened a newspaper front page with the teaser: "Is this a boy or a girl? Only seven people on earth know for sure. And they're not telling" (Poisson A1, 26-27). Eighty thousand hits on the first day made it the "most read" *Toronto Star* article in its online history.[2] An international media frenzy and public response followed, along with discussions that continue to this day.

YOU CAN'T BE NEUTRAL ON A MOVING TRAIN (ZINN)[3]

The owner wraps our falafels in wax paper and says, "Don't worry, I'll make sure you know which is which." On mine, the marker squeaks out, 'spicy'. I smirk. I'm turning forty and that wouldn't be the descriptor I'd reach for. With the same permanent blue pen, I watch the other two receive labels: G (for Girl) and B (for Boy). Jazz pipes up, "Mine has G for great." Kio looks puzzled. "Do you think B is for beautiful?" I consider it as we walk home, carrying Storm. "I think that's for you to decide," I finally conclude. It's the start of another important conversation. There's no such thing as an easy dinner.

This moment does not offer a neutral way forward. For any parent. Neutrality isn't possible in parenting or with gender. Gender is a social experiment[4] and *every* parenting choice, labelled or not, active or omitted, sensationalized or condoned, refines a child's world view and has an impact on how they grow, learn and define themselves and others. The best evidence suggests that today's limited gender framework will have negative health and social impacts on all children[5]—not just mine, who self-determine in a way that defies categorization as Boy or Girl. The truth is that essentializing gender into a binary hurts everyone. I want to bear witness to the impact of the game our kids are signed up for. In Storm's words, "Snaa Feeer!" ("It's not fair!"). My children need support to stand up to a culture that talks the talk about inclusion but condones homophobia, transphobia, sexism, racism, classism and ableism. The question is: how can I parent in ways that protect my child's right to a safe, creative and healthy future?

WE'RE FISH IN CONFORMITY'S WATER

Her child and mine are wet and unwilling to move on. They play together on the bridge over a creek. She's a stranger, bemused when I decline to assign gender to my six-week-old baby. She mentions, laughing, that her daughter's Montreal daycare asked her two-year-old to wear skirts instead of leggings to "fit in better with the girls." Giant splatters of mud and a huge smile now adorn her daughter. When mom's eyes follow, there is a gasp before the child is doused in water, extinguishing the grin and uncovering a frilled pink skirt.

An accepted child-rearing paradigm is teaching conformity. The institution of the family is the first nursery where gender is planted in a child's socially sensitive brain; a brain, science proposes, that wires itself "in response to its own experience" (Eliot 6). Mothers-to-be croon to round bellies, but unwittingly characterize even fetal movements according to known sex (Rothman 130).[6] Social convention encourages non-consultative gender assignment based on physiology and repeated rehearsal of the allocated gender (It's a boy! Good girl! What a big boy! What a beautiful girl!). I appointed gender to my first-born based on genital endowment. I announced it to friends and family, even in polite conversation during the early years. I was wrong. Maybe the marathon breastfeeding also befuddled the resistance I had planned to the hypnotic overload of gendered toys,[7] books and clothing.

Jazz could sign but not speak when she picked out a pink feather boa at a thrift store. The cashier refused to sell the two-dollar item to a 'boy'. A few years later, a convenience store owner smiled and handed a transit pass over the counter, along with an unsolicited rant at Kio about his responsibility to protect his older sister. Before the young brain can codify memory or conjure words, conformity to gender is embedded deeply enough to evade conscious questioning. At the playground, three-year-old gender disciplinarians are satisfied that Jazz cannot self identify as a boy, have long hair, like pink or play midwife *"because boys don't."*

LESSONS IN "GOING ALONG TO GET ALONG"

By the summer of 2011, I was wearied by sweet-talk messages from NBC, ABC, *Dr. Phil, the Oprah Winfrey Network, television stations in France and radio shows in Australia, Al Jazeera and People Magazine, documentary makers and even a collector from Peoria, Illinois who wondered if we were selling autographed photos. A message got through from a local mother searching for support. We met at a café and she told me about her eight-year-old son who loved to don skirts and tall boots at home. He mustered the courage to go glam on Pink Day,[8] codified by his school board as the assigned time for supporting diversity. That morning, he pulled on a pink, spaghetti-strap dress and left the house smiling. The school principal visited the child's classroom to berate him and tell him to remove the dress.[9] When his mom organized a meeting to discuss gender diversity, parents voiced support for the administrator, who didn't feel an apology to the shaken youngster was necessary. It was the child's first direct encounter with the school principal, having never been "in trouble" before.*

My children are unschooled.[10] Partly it's because I'm worried that institutions like schools unabashedly continue the family's work as society's stealthy thugs imposing gender conformity. At the Pride parade in Toronto, Canada, a woman in our handful of walkers turned to my family to say, "I feel lonely down here." She wanted to be with the hundred people in a truck following us, bearing the slogan, "The Toronto District School Board supports equity for all." The TDSB is the largest school board in Canada and the fourth largest in North America, made up of 600 schools, 260,000 students and 37,000 employees ("About the TDSB"). I don't need help from my mathematician partner to see (and feel) that it's a slim fraction of the community hitting the pavement to show LGBTTIQQ2SA [11] students that their six-hour day is spent with others who celebrate the diversity of who they are.

Despite research showing that "early child and brain development sets trajectories in health, learning and behaviour for life" (Mustard 11), conformity training at school continues to undermine the development of pro-social skills, valuing diversity and independent thinking in children. For the very young, diaper changes teach narrow categorization: truck motifs for 'boys' and pink princesses for 'girls'. A blushing daycare worker stammered an extended apology to my friend and her daughter when the "girl" nappies ran out and the child went home wearing a "boy" one. Grouping by binary gender is enforced in elementary school for bathroom breaks and line-ups. My family visited a local school where grade one students needed less than five minutes to generate an accurate list of the contents in dollar-store loot bags. Without a peek, they knew that the bag *"For a boy"* would have toy guns, fast vehicles and action figurines and the one *"For a girl"* would include jewellery, dolls and hair clips.[12] Six-year-olds could articulate the message: girls are supposed to be caretakers and cultivate beauty. Boys need to embrace aggression, risk taking and power dominance to express masculinity. When one of David's grade seven students took the initiative to do a web search for examples of "boy toys," the results were links to images of scantily clad girls and women. *Toronto Sun* columnist Joe Warmington, summarized it succinctly: eight-year-olds should "think what their parents and teachers tell them to think." And it's a bit scary.

THE DOCUMENTED DOWNSIDE OF CONFORMITY

Jazz stands tall like a gymnast rounding up a perfect ten. She (still using he) shows off tights, topped with a short puffed-sleeve shirt, to accentuate the bright knitted frills, stripes and flowers. I stutter that tights are worn under other garments. Jazz explains that tights are leggings and socks as one, pointing out that it's a pragmatic shortcut to the tiresome complexity of getting ready. Then she spins on her heel, dispelling the spectre I've raised of playmates responding to this strong stand of self-determination. She tears down the hall after a giggling Kio. They're helping Storm choose and pull on clothes s(he) has chosen. Despite the unexpected eruption of my own conformity training, I've failed to extinguish the joyful independence my children bring to everyday tasks like getting dressed. I've been given another chance to (re)learn.

What helps me let go of relying on *"this is what you should or shouldn't do"* is fifty years of science documenting the dark side of human conformity. The pursuit of tidy hair and matching socks correlates to other tendencies too. Famous pioneering social psychology studies demonstrated decades ago that people in groups will imitate aggression (Bandura), assimilate to the crowd's error even when knowing better (Asch), comply with violent instructions from an authority (Milgram), harm others based on arbitrary role assignment (Haney, Banks and Zimbardo) and incline toward discriminatory (Tajfel) and even assaultive behaviour (Sherif et al.). If very current, highly publicized, real-world examples of lynching, gang rape and genocide aren't a convincing indictment of teaching kids to follow the group's lead, I look to research by Meier, Hinsz and Heimerdinger in 2007. Their study found that groups commit more aggression than individuals *who are thinking for themselves* (my added words and emphasis).

Group-on-group contexts beget the most aggression (Meier and Hinsz), which is why imposed binary categorization is dangerous to children (and all people). Girl/Boy is but one false binary that misrepresents diversity by way of oversimplification—Young/Old; Straight/Gay; Rich/Poor; Able/Disabled; and White/Black are others. The claim that sorting by physiology (or 'sex') creates an immutable two-category reality is a bit laughable. But that aside, why don't we teach children that gender refers to expectations "that a *given society* considers appropriate" (WHO, *www.who.int*)? Gender is literally a set of arbitrary rules *made up* by dominant adults for the purpose of maintaining power differentials. Children can see that the lion's share is for Boys, much less for Girls, and that it's foolhardy (or very courageous) to define outside the binary altogether. Children should learn that the gender status quo *changes* based on historical period, geography, family environment, community, culture and context. It's valid to question why gender can't be the individual's to define.

IN THE DARK

Late one winter night my neighbour rings our doorbell after dark. She swells with pride and turns her cheek for a thank-you kiss as she pushes an unsolicited four-piece suit into Jazz's hands. She is matter-of-fact, "Wear this and you'll feel more like a little man." Jazz shrugs, "Why do I want to?" By now, Jazz knows there's no such thing as a free suit.

My worry-monster is unruly. We live in a society that sees the expression of difference as "going too far" and responds punitively or—too often—with violence. Even by preschool, peers express "distinctly cooler responses" to children who play in "gender-inappropriate ways" (Fine 218). Harvard researchers have documented a one-in-ten risk of abuse "perpetrated by parents or other adults in the home" (Roberts et al.) against children expressing themselves outside what is expected from their biological sex. When lead author Andrea Roberts was interviewed, she acknowledged a "lasting impact on health" (Findlay) associated with the elevated risk for Post Traumatic Stress Syndrome (PTSS) in non conformers—after all, they're more likely to experience "poorer relationships with parents, peer rejection, harassment, and physical and verbal victimization" (Roberts et al. 415). At a community Farmer's Market, Jazz and I just hug when the kids she'd rallied into a rousing game of tag stop mid-game. One child, pigtails and sun-yellow skirt flouncing, had erupted into sudden indignation and ripped Jazz's favourite dress (because boys shouldn't have one). No parent wants to send their child with a kiss into the face of intolerance or misunderstanding.[13] Do they?

I shore up my commitment to honour my child's own choices by remembering that conformity to the gender binary will not protect them. Children within the binary are not safe. One statistic estimates that "80 percent of adolescents" will "experience some type of gender-based bullying before graduating from high school," a problem associated with "increased rates of depression, anxiety, academic withdrawal, lower academic performance and suicide" (Anagnostopoulos et al. 3). Television, billboards, children's magazine ads, food packaging, and the banners on preschool internet sites market gender as an "either/or" designation that restricts friendship (girls or boys), colour preference (pink or blue), interests (sports or shopping), aspirations (princess or action hero) and attire (frills or cargo pants). The malignancy grows when parents, trained as gender stealth-marketers, feel compelled to communicate narrow, top-down gender expectations. Research suggests that children "who feel they have to fulfill certain conditions in order to win their parents' approval may end up not liking themselves" (Kohn 23). At a gym birthday party for my friend's three-year-old, a dad swooped in (smiling) to snatch up his preschool son as he darted toward a pink soccer ball—"after all, he is a boy! And there are blue ones!" Children know that gender allocation also defines worth. In a 2001 study, children shown pictures of people doing unfamiliar jobs consistently rated the ones performed by men as "more difficult, better paid and more important" (Liben, Bigler and Krogh). Binary gender presents a challenge to *every* child's freedom, safety and self actualization.

Just like in *The Dark*, a storybook Kio loves about a spooky blob that flumps onto the kitchen table one morning, binary gender has grown uncontrollably huge by gobbling up every shadow in the neighbourhood. In the Robert Munsch tale, darkness falls on everyone, even parents who stumble into the backyard and can't find a way back in. Until Jule Ann—one smart kid full of courage—tricks the Dark back into a cookie jar and throws it into a garbage truck, locked with glue and tape. So, which healthy parenting strategies can take the place of the existing gender status quo? My smart, gender non-conforming kids full of courage have ideas, thank goodness (because I'm still fumbling in the backyard). I had to help with spelling when Jazz, at four years old, hatched the idea to write a book and sell it at a local bookstore to raise money for a women's shelter. The concluding page said, "Let your kids be whoever they are." Since we're in the dark, I believe the only safe way out is to listen carefully. And love a lot.

We bike down the path to gymnastics a few times a week so that each of my three can have a class with a well-loved coach named Suzi. Suzi smiles slyly at Storm because she just "can't wait to *know*." Sometimes, it makes me feel like a contestant on a game show or the unwitting subject of a reality TV program. One day, a newly diaper-less Storm turned a somersault right out of a pair of red sweatpants. With a whoop, Suzi pounced, "A-ha! Girl underwear!" I laughed earnestly. Storm was wearing a pair of Jazz's underwear, filched from our giant communal underwear bin. I retold the story later and Jazz giggled, saying "Tell Suzi not to judge a book by its underwear!"

GLIMMER—NO, BONFIRE—OF HOPE

If history is a worthy teacher, it seems that our non-conforming children may have important things to say. Among the bragging rights of past non-conformers are achievements that have brought us more justice, better health and a higher quality of life. Without them, we'd be missing antibiotics. And weekends. Women would still be languishing without the vote. Racial inequality would continue to be institutionalized in slavery. No one would be talking about how to stop Global Warming. Lesbians and gay men wouldn't be celebrating marriage. There would be less music, art, poetry, and not as many edgy films or live performances. More trans people would be hiding. Progress comes from thinking outside the box.

More importantly, when people challenge the mainstream, knee jerk responses expose the reality of the status quo. A week after our stumble onto the media stage with Storm, a member of the local vigilante public slowed his car beside me and my children to spit out a theory: "BOY!" Tragicomic moments in parenting can be transformative. Just like a meditation bell, it rang clear to my children as evidence that sometimes adults make mistakes. Kio wrinkled his brow, commenting "Did that person call *Jazz* a boy?" Everyone laughed. Later on a bus-stop bench, our questioning deepened into why the person we had encountered had been angry. It's an activity we enjoy—practicing alternate perspectives. First, we share our experience of a situation. Then we explore a myriad of possible explanations for the other person's choices. My kids love generating intricate life stories for people. I enjoy the tale-making because it encourages a complicated understanding of situations and interferes with the habit of taking things personally. Excellent practice for thinking independently. Around that time, all sorts of opinions were arriving (skillfully and unskillfully) from very surprising places. As Barbara Colouroso[14] predicted, it looked just like crisis, but actually was a disguised opportunity to find a like-minded community (of children *and* adults). What an immeasurable gift, this proof that sometimes you *do* need to put your face into the storm to find unexpected allies. All told, the path of the non-conformer may not be the easiest one, but it has much to commend it.

My first two children acquired the words "Dad," "Dog," and a few dozen others before any name for me emerged. So it was an unexpected ode to motherhood when I heard Storm intone "Mum" just after a year. My heart felt full. The story becomes more beau-

tiful. At eighteen months, Storm had already been saying "Dad" for a few weeks, when one day, I watched with some mixture of amusement and stunned curiosity as Storm addressed David. "Mom, annie urse?" which translates to, "Mom, another nurse." Storm was asking David to breastfeed! Without hesitation, he cuddled Storm in a nursing position, and a tiny nose tucked itself into David's naked breast. With closed eyes, adult and child were lost in a close embrace for two full minutes. Then Storm climbed down to toddle off full speed and find a new adventure. From that day to this, Storm uses the word "Mom" not to imply a gendered role, but to describe a source of nurturance that can come from any adult with a mind open enough to offer it. Neither of my other children showed much surprise. They did not drag out any exasperated physiological explanation for why nursing with a Dad is impossible. I hope it's a sign that they feel empowered to opt out of norms if it happens that there's a healthier way to get their needs met.

There's tremendous untapped creative power in children's diversification of the gender landscape. We're busy generating new labels (like gender fluid, gender creative or gender independent), organizing task forces and discussing gender non-conformity as if it's an outbreak. While trained professionals in the twenty-first century write; "yes, a new pediatric problem is in town" (Meyer 571), the real courage of gender-creative children unfolds. Gender non-conformity is not a problem to fix. These children are sidelining a dangerous status quo, risking censure to express a diversity that promises to transform the rigid teeter totter of binary gender into a more inclusive, joyful roundabout. Agency and freedom of expression are *that* important to being human, and gender non-conforming children are sticking up for *everyone's* right to both. The Search Institute's developmental assets framework names forty markers of healthy development in children, including self esteem, integrity, honesty, and personal power (Scales et al). Empirical research suggests that children with those internal assets (and external assets like family support) will be more likely to thrive.

I watch my non-conformers observe the status quo (what's outside), acknowledge with confidence personal preferences, thoughts, feelings and interests (what's inside) and synthesize the two into responsible, self-honouring choices. Not always, but enough that

I understand that these skills would be useful to *all* children. It's novel to see children gather empowerment in a way that doesn't rely on obtaining it through denying others a fair share. I'm amazed to see young gender non-conformers practice a Red Cross violence prevention adage that I used to teach to adults: *Talk* (speak up for what you believe); *Walk* (find a safe space); and *Squawk* (find someone who will support you). These skills are at the core of the best expensive, adult written anti-bullying resources being purchased by parents, teachers and community members desperate to curb unnecessary hurt. And our gender independent children have them already. In bucketfuls.

ME TOO PLEASE

My three children are giggling helplessly. Storm arrives in the kitchen, grabs my arm and drags me into the playroom, saying, "Mom, waatch." When I stumble in, all three jump up, hissing like pythons and miming giant arcs of pee all over the room. "You pee!" says the littlest one, as the pretend pissing match dissolves into snorts of laughter. They have tears streaming down their faces as mom joins in.

I'm grateful that my children have made a place for me in their revolution. It's no neutral spot. Shifting into neutral is an emergency measure for when you're slipping headlong into a crash collision or ricocheting off a bridge into frigid waters. It's a vain pitch for a modicum of control. This moment, as the discussion about gender creativity gains momentum, feels important. Like if we get it wrong, there *is* a risk of sliding off the road. So now is the time to take a stand and believe in our own—but especially our children's—agency. Parents are placed at the front line of social influence, which admittedly is a chaotic spot to be intentional. But parenting must be the future we suggest by the principles we model. Which ones then? Raising feminist sons and daughters addresses inequities, but may depend too much on a two-team foundation—an oversimplification that makes differential power assignment *that* much easier. Plus, where are the feminist parenting strategies for a once-son, now-daughter? Gender neutral parenting feels like an oxymoron, suggesting the impossible notion of gender as non-partisan. Here's my "radical parenting strategy"— I'm trying to listen. Sounds boring, so David and I made up a fancy name. We call it *gender engaged parenting*.

ROLLING UP OUR SLEEVES

Gender engaged parenting facilitates a child's conscious interchange with their world, for the purpose of growing *the child's* capacity to make their own healthy choices. John Taylor Gatto warns: "suppressing [a child's] involvement in society—on thin and specious psychological grounds—is an unforgivable crime" (11).[15] Gender is a big part of the real-world. It is a socially significant venue where children have the right to express their true selves, in an esteemed and responsible way. To protect their agency, children need practice in *questioning* everyday limits to their expression, limits that are everywhere. Shopping for rain boots in a world of pink or blue; Dora or Diego; action heroes or princesses can lead to discussion about capitalist strangleholds on a child's freedom to express a unique identity. Children need to know that they are targeted consumers in a profit-game of branding social status-quos like gender.

When Kio *really* wanted a pink dress adorned with Disney's Tinkerbell, we sat down on the store's dusty floor to talk about multinationals, marketing and media representations of women. After our chat, he spent all his money and wore the dress for four weeks straight, until the images wore completely off. Holding open space for children to make their own choices requires letting kids think for themselves, instead of reinforcing that adults know best. Later, Kio was patient (even attentive) when we read together sections of Peggy Ornstein's *Cinderella Ate My Daughter*, although admittedly he continues to love Tinkerbell. Gender provides a wealth of opportunity for children's interest in questioning limits and understanding the whys of everything. Is boy *really* the opposite of girl? Should people be restricted to *either/or?* What possibilities does *both/and* offer? When parents foster engagement with real aspects of a child's world, choice that was previously obscured in the monolithic status quo becomes visible. Curious inquiry highlights the true diversity of options beyond narrow and branded binaries like Girl/Boy. Ah, freedom!

Jazz is holding onto No Ordinary Day, *a book that was a birth-day gift. She says, "I want to write to Deborah Ellis." "Why?" I ask. "To tell her I like her stories," Jazz answers. "What do you like about her stories?" I pose. "I like that it's real—there is Afghanistan. There is the Taliban. There is leprosy. These are true people. So I can know about it and do something."*

Fostering meaningful and healthy choice-making requires helping children understand and subvert power misuse. Without knowing how binary gender works to maintain unfair differential power and aggression, children will continue to conform to a gender status quo that erodes their freedom and limits their potential. They'll believe adults blathering about how "girls and boys can be whatever they want.[16] It isn't true (not even for those who *do* identify as Girl or Boy).

If self-determination was reality, what explanation can we provide for the influence that gender allocation has on socioeconomic status, the likelihood of experiencing violence, and bluntly, the probability of survival? If girls and boys can be whatever they want, and if it really *is* okay to be whoever you *are*, then why did the international media and a host of fear-mongering psychologists, ethicists and social workers spend weeks worrying publicly about a five-year-old "allowed" to wear dresses or a baby given the privacy and agency to disclose sex and gender when *they* chose. Implying that gender is a fair game robs children of *understanding* the *very* real challenges that binary gender will present to them. Likewise, offering "gender neutral" choices fails to expose the power imbalance that's in place. A child that doesn't know that gender normative behaviours support a system that divides people into *more powerful* or *less powerful (Oppressor or Oppressed)* doesn't easily have the power to choose differently. Clear knowledge empowers children to protect themselves (and others) by refusing to conform to a harmful status quo.

FREEDOM IS THE RIGHT TO TELL PEOPLE WHAT THEY DO NOT WANT TO HEAR[17]

There are times when I'm not sure it's possible to be more exhausted. Times when even my tear ducts are too tired to work. Right inside a moment like that, Storm bit my breast while nursing. Hard. There was a blasting "NO!" Jazz read this vignette and called me on an omission in it, so I admit (grudgingly) that I flumped—none too gently—that eighteen-month-old child with the large teeth onto the couch beside me. Jazz, eyes wide, demanded, "Why did you do that?" "Because I'm really HURT!" was my poor excuse. She considered it for a minute. Then firmly, "Mom, an eye for an eye makes the whole world blind." Infuriatingly true.

Teaching children about power allows them to challenge its misuse. It's the next step to democratize the family and reject the institutionalized power imbalance between parents and children. Empowered kids demand a purge of parental lapses into convenient authoritarianism. The hard work of collabouration and principle-driven problem solving begins. The result: a conscious queering of parenting, strongly anchored in the meaningful and inalienable rights and responsibilities of parent *and* child. Critics love to typify this as failing to provide boundaries (Porter), but in fact, it's maintaining firm limits in places of greatest importance (health, safety and kindness) and otherwise nurturing agency. As an example, we are all accountable to two rules in our family: 1) Be kind to self and others, and 2) Do what you can do for the common good (of family, community and the world). Facilitating these limits requires all the parenting energy we can muster, even given the elimination of power struggles over getting a haircut, eating everything on your plate or saying sorry when you don't mean it. In the venue of gender, it translates into protecting each person's right to self determine. We avoid telling anyone in the family how to feel, who to be or what to look like. That alone is a full time job.

CALL TO ACTION

Last week, while I facilitated a breastfeeding support group, Jazz made a necklace for me. When I put it on, she pointed out the letters—MOM— centered in front. For a moment, Jazz was disappointed that the letters were upside down. Until she realized that the necklace said MOM to me, when I looked down and WOW to everyone else. "That's what the world thinks of you, Mom—WOW."

34

I wore a Cheshire grin for three days. I wished I had told her. I don't care what the world thinks, Jazz. I care what you think.

I looked up parenting in the dictionary. I was surprised to find that it said *noun*. I say it's time for revision. Gender engaged parenting is definitely a *verb*. In the short term, it's about honouring my children's agency. In the long run, I hope it contributes to making parenting into the joyful social movement it needs to be, with the potential to create a fairer world. When I'm terrified—feeling the moment at the top of the upswing when my stomach starts to flip—I look at David's painting (or call on his patience and care). I remember Deborah Ellis, a youth author I admire, saying, "When I'm able to consider that the work I want to do is more important than the fear I have of doing the work, then I'm able to move forward and do what I feel I need to do." ("Shannon Skinner"). Small risks can make big ripples. Like giving your baby a little respite from the gender onslaught.

Research by Jost and colleagues found that parents are slightly more likely to place a birth announcement in the newspaper for a boy than for a girl—but it's the footnote that gives me hope. The statistically significant difference disappeared in families where the mother had not taken the father's last name (Jost, Pelham and Carvallo qtd. in Fine 195). While this correlation is of tiny speculative importance to scientists, it stands out to me as encouragement that small acts with deep philosophical roots are powerful indeed. At the top of the upswing, I'm gripping the plastic covered chains and taking my cues from the smart gender-sceptics in my home. I need to be decisive. If I choose to experience the exhilaration of the journey, to celebrate and support my children, I'm betting that the momentum of it will pull me face first into the sky—and smack into the world I dream of for my children. And yours.

[1]David Stocker is the artist; also my partner, co-conspirator and the most patient and talented person and activist that I know. He's Jazz, Kio and Storm's dad, a teacher at an alternative school, and the author of a book called *MaththatMatters: A Teacher Resource Linking Math and Social Justice*.

[2]Thestar.com has more on the viral response to the original arti-

cle about our family. For example: "Anatomy of a Hit: How the Genderless Baby Story Became thestar.com's Most Read Story of All Time."

[3]This is the title of Howard Zinn's 1994 autobiographical book about years of working for social change. It's irresistible to quote as an articulation that every choice influences our world. It's a hopeful reminder to be intentional and justice-supporting.

[4]The World Health Organization defines gender as the "roles, behaviours, activities and attributes that a given society considers appropriate" in the article entitled "What Do We Mean by 'Sex'and 'Gender'?"

[5]Negative social and health impacts have been documented for girls and boys, for those within the binary and for non-conformers. Peggy Orenstein's *Cinderella Ate My Daughter* provides a review of the impact on girls. It's sobering to see findings linking "exposure to sexualized female ideals with lower self esteem, negative mood, and depressive symptoms among adolescent girls" (*Report of the APA Task Force* 24). Moreover, "studies show that teenage girls and college students who hold conventional views about femininity ...are less ambitious and more likely to be depressed than peers" (Orenstein 16). Masculinity's no picnic either. Jackson Katz is able to articulate that violence, with obvious negative health and social consequences for both perpetrator and victim, is an intrinsic aspect of socialized masculinity. His book, *The Macho Paradox* or his older film, *Tough Guise* are convincing, even without going as far as looking at Michael Kimmel's work, in particular a 2006 co-written article linking masculinity, homophobia and school shootings. Sadly, there's too much evidence to list about the ways in which the gender status quo is also hurting non-conformers. Succinctly put, "in many parts of the world, having a trans identity still puts a person at risk of discrimination, violence and even death" (Whittle xi). Children are not protected. Research from the Harvard School of Public Health found that "childhood gender non-conformity has been associated with an array of childhood psychosocial stressors, including poorer relationships with parents, peer rejection, harassment and physical and verbal victimization" (Roberts et al. 415). Lead researcher Andrea Roberts told *The Toronto Star* that "discrimination against gender non-conformity

affects one in ten kids, affects kids at a very young age, and has lasting impacts on health" (Findlay). If you need convincing that society is enforcing the restrictive binary (as opposed to innate biology playing itself out), read Cordelia Fine's book *Delusions of Gender*. She debunks the "gaps, assumptions, inconsistencies, poor methodologies and leaps of faith" (xxvii) inherent in the neuro-scientific excuses for gender stereotyping. Then she exposes the brain-altering clout of socialization to gender that we impose on infants and young children. Further discussion of the "surprisingly little solid evidence of sex differences in children's brains" (5) pours out of *Pink Brain, Blue Brain* by Lise Eliot. The research is clear: binary gender has negative outcomes and we're the ones driving the car (recklessly).

[6]Sociobiologist Barbara Rothman found that mothers described the movements of their unborn babies differently based on knowledge of their sex: males were "vigorous" and "strong" and females were "not excessively energetic, not terribly active" (130).

[7]See Fine (page 198) for a description of Alison Nash and Rosemary Krawczyk's 1994 toy inventory. They found that even among babies six to twelve months old, boys had more vehicles and machines while girls had more dolls and housekeeping toys.

[8]In Nova Scotia, Canada in 2007, two grade twelve students organized friends (who spread the word until hundreds participated) to wear pink to support a younger student who had been bullied at school for sporting a pink shirt. That prompted the Toronto District School Board to establish a Pink Day, in which students are encouraged to "wear pink in support of diversity" and school communities are invited to "hold events and activities that will engage their community and challenge gender stereotypes" ("International Day of Pink").

[9]The incident happened in 2011 at a school in Toronto, Canada. The boy was asked to leave his classroom and was forced to remove the dress. Although the administrator later conceded that he was not behaving disrespectfully in the dress, she still felt that his choice would trigger inappropriate behaviours from other students.

[10]Unschooling is an approach to education that emphasizes real-world, child-led, self-directed opportunities for learning. Many people typify it as a type of homeschooling, but unschooling may

be as different from homeschooling as it is from institutionalized schooling. Educator John Holt is an important voice for unschoolers and his website defines unschooling as "allowing children as much freedom to learn in the world, as their parents can comfortably bear" (Farenga). Unschoolers learn through every-day life, including play, household tasks, personal interests, work, social interaction and contribution, but traditionally do not rely on paper-and-pencil, school-based curriculum and/or grading systems.

[11]Lesbian, Gay, Bisexual, Transsexual, Transgender, Intersex, Queer, Questioning, 2-Spirited and Allies.

[12]In June 2011, our family (Jazz, Kio and Storm included) visited *The Grove Alternative Community School* in Toronto, Canada to talk about gender. We took *"For a girl"* and *"For a boy"* party loot bags, purchased from a dollar store. David and I have repeated this activity with hundreds of people of all ages over the last decade in workshops. It always yields the same results, which is a bit spooky.

[13]I don't want to contribute to the societal confusion that conflates sexuality and gender but it feels important to make a note here. It's a popular (not factual) idea that it will protect young people to suppress the gender or sexuality they wish to express. The rationale is that open expression of minority behaviours make youth vulnerable to harm. So, a recent *Toronto Star* article (and the research it references) is of interest. It demonstrates that, compared to those who haven't "come out," "declared lesbians, gays and bisexuals have lower stress hormone levels and fewer symptoms of anxiety, depression and burnout." The study "also finds that gay and bisexual men are healthier than their heterosexual counterparts" (Boyle A15). Why? Lead author Robert-Paul Juster postulates that it may be because "the stress of coming out can make you resilient to future stress" (Boyle A15). I acknowledge that the research deals with sexuality and not gender expression. Still, it suggests that being yourself is important to your health. And although it's difficult to be different, being who you are is healthier than maintaining a "false self" (Kohn 23).

[14]Barbara Colouroso is an internationally recognized parenting expert, author of five books, including four best sellers. She phoned me personally to offer support in the first weeks of the media uproar around our family, and offered wisdom on surviving an

organized social response to standing up for peace, particularly when the media is involved. Her book, *Kids are Worth It*, is a parenting "go-to" in our home.

[15]I replaced the word "student" with the word "child" for clarity here. The quote is from John Taylor Gatto's new book, *The Guerilla Curriculum: How to Take Education in Spite of Schooling*, as quoted in *Home Education Magazine*.

[16]This "boys and girls can do anything" mantra is directly quoted in a recent *Globe and Mail* article (Balkissoon) and is frustratingly attributed as *the* goal for all parents affirming gender non-conforming children.

[17]This quote is attributed to George Orwell.

WORKS CITED

"About the TDSB." *Toronto District School Board*. Web. 25 Aug. 2013.

"Anatomy of a Hit: How the Genderless Baby Story Became thestar.com's Most Read Story of All Time." *The Toronto Star* 28 May 2011: IN4. Print.

Anagnostopoulos, D., N. T. Buchanan, C. Pereira, and L. F. Lichty. "School Staff Responses to Gender-Based Bullying as Moral Interpretation: An Exploratory Study." *Educational Policy* 23.4 (2009): 519-53. Print.

Asch, S. E. "Opinions and Social Pressure." *Scientific American* 193 (1955): 31-35. Print.

Balkissoon, Denise. "How Do You Parent a Transgendered Kid?" *Globe and Mail* 11 Jan. 2013. Web. 12 Jan. 2013.

Bandura, A., Dorothea Ross, and Sheila A. Ross. "Transmission of Aggression through Imitation of Aggressive Models." *The Journal of Abnormal and Social Psychology* 63.3 (1961): 575-82. Print.

Boyle, Theresa. "Coming out of the closet a healthy choice, study finds." *The Toronto Star* 30 Jan. 2013: A1, A15. Print.

Canadian Red Cross. *Challenge Abuse Through Respect Education (C.A.R.E) Resource Guide*. Vancouver: RespectED: Violence and Abuse Prevention Program, 2002. Print.

Colouroso, Barbara. *Kids Are Worth It! Giving Your Child the Gift of Inner Discipline*. New York: W. Morrow, 1994. Print.

Eliot, Lise. *Pink Brain, Blue Brain: How Small Differences Grow into Troublesome Gaps and What We Can Do about It*. Boston: Houghton Mifflin Harcourt, 2009. Print.

Ellis, Deborah. *No Ordinary Day*. Toronto: Groundwood, 2011. Print.

Farenga, Pat. "Unschooling." *Growing Without Schooling*. John Holt. Web. 26 Jan. 2013.

Findlay, Stephanie. "Children Who Are Gender Nonconforming at Greater Risk of Abuse: Harvard Study." *The Toronto Star*. 20 Feb. 2012. Web. 15 July 2012.

Fine, Cordelia. *Delusions of Gender: How Our Minds, Society, and Neurosexism Create Difference*. New York: W. W. Norton, 2010. Print.

Gatto, John Taylor. "We Need Adventure More Than We Need Algebra." *Home Education Magazine* 30.1 (January-February 2013): 10-11. Print.

Haney, C., Banks, W. C. and P. G. Zimbardo. "A Study of Prisoners and Guards in a Simulated Prison." *Naval Research Review* 30 (1973): 4-17. Print.

"International Day of Pink." *Toronto District School Board*. Web. 02 Jan. 2013.

Juster, Robert-Paul, Nathan Grant Smith, Emilie Ouellet, Shireen Sindi, and Sonja J. Lupien. "Sexual Orientation and Disclosure in Relation to Psychiatric Symptoms." *Psychosomatic Medicine* 75 (2013): 1-14. American Psychosomatic Society, 29 Jan. 2013. Web. 1 Feb. 2013.

Katz, Jackson. *The Macho Paradox: Why Some Men Hurt Women and How All Men Can Help*. Naperville, IL: Source, 2006. Print.

Kimmel, Michael S. and Matthew Mahler. "Adolescent Masculinity, Homophobia, and Violence: Random School Shootings, 1982-2001." *American Behavioural Scientist* 46.10 (2003): 1439-458. Print.

Kohn, Alfie. *Unconditional Parenting: Moving from Rewards and Punishments to Love and Reason*. New York: Atria, 2005. Print.

Liben, Lynn S., Rebecca S. Bigler, and Holleen R. Krogh. "Pink and Blue Collar Jobs: Children's Judgments of Job Status and Job Aspirations in Relation to Sex of Worker." *Journal of Experimental Child Psychology* 79.4 (2001): 346-63. Print.

Meier, Brian P., Verlin B. Hinsz, and Sarah R. Heimerdinger. "A Framework for Explaining Aggression Involving Groups." *Social and Personality Psychology Compass* 1.1 (2007): 298-312. Print.

Meier, Brian P., and Verlin B. Hinsz. "A Comparison of Human Aggression Committed by Groups and Individuals: An Interindividual–intergroup Discontinuity." *Journal of Experimental Social Psychology* 40.4 (2004): 551-59. Print.

Meyer, Walter J. "Gender Identity Disorder: An Emerging Problem for Pediatricians." *Pediatrics*. 20 Feb. 2012. Web. 2 Apr. 2012.

Milgram, Stanley. *Obedience to Authority: An Experimental View*. New York: Harper & Row, 1974. Print.

Munsch, Robert. *The Dark*. Toronto: Annick Press, 1997. Print.

Mustard, J. F. "A Message from the Authors." Preface. *Early Years Study 2: Putting Science into Action*. By Margaret Norrie. McCain and Stuart Shanker. Toronto, Ont.: Council for Early Child Development, March 2007. Web. Aug. 10 2011.

Orenstein, Peggy. *Cinderella Ate My Daughter: Dispatches from the Front Lines of the New Girlie-girl Culture*. New York, NY: HarperCollins, 2011. Print.

Poisson, Jayme. "Footloose and gender-free." *The Toronto Star* 21 May 2011: A1, 26-27. Print.

Porter, C. "Firestorm of judgment." *The Toronto Star* 25 May 2011: E1. Print.

Report of the APA Task Force on the Sexualization of Girls. American Psychological Association, 2010. Web. 15 Sept. 2012.

Roberts, A. L., H. L. Corliss, K. C. Koenen and S. B. Austin. "Childhood Gender Nonconformity: A Risk Indicator for Childhood Abuse and Post Traumatic Stress in Youth." *Pediatrics* 129.3 (2012): 410-17. Print.

Rothman, Barbara Katz. *The Tentative Pregnancy: Prenatal Diagnosis and the Future of Motherhood*. London: Pandora, 1988. Print.

Scales, Peter, Arturo Sesma, and Brent Bolstrom. *Coming into Their Own: How Developmental Assets Promote Positive Growth in Middle Childhood*. Minneapolis, MN: Search Institute, 2004. Print.

"Shannon Skinner Interviews Author Deborah Ellis." ThatMedia, 2012. Web. 29 Jan. 2013.

Sherif, M., O. J. Harvey, B. J. White, W. Hood and C. W. Sherif. *Intergroup Conflict and Cooperation: The Robbers Cave Experiment.* Norman, OK: The University Book Exchange, 1961. 155-184. Print.

Tajfel, H. "Experiments in Intergroup Discrimination." *Scientific American* 223 (1970): 96-102. Print.

Warmington, Joe. "Kids Should Be Educated, Not Indoctrinated." *The Toronto Sun.* 8 May 2012. Web. 22 June 2012.

Whittle, Stephen. "Foreword." *The Transgender Studies Reader.* Ed. Susan Stryker and Stephen Whittle. New York: Routledge, 2006. xi-xvi. Print.

World Health Organization (WHO). "What Do We Mean by 'Sex' and 'Gender'?" Web. 22 Jan. 2013.

2.
Get Your Gender Binary
Off My Childhood!

Towards a Movement for Children's Gender Self-Determination

JANE WARD

CHILDHOOD GENDER FLUIDITY received significant media attention in 2011 and 2012. *The Boston Globe* covered the story of Nicole, a transgendered child of initially heartbroken parents who now embrace Nicole's gender identity (English). *New York Magazine* ran a story about the parents of four trans children, including Molly, who was assigned male at birth and began telling her parents that she was a girl at age three (Green). Several major media outlets also featured Storm, a baby born in Toronto to parents who decided not to assign a sex or gender to their child, but to let Storm determine, when ready, how to identify.

As a queer parent and scholar, I was struck as I read these stories by what they reveal about the ways that queer and transgender movement discourses are being (mis)understood and operationalized by parents, doctors, and psychotherapists—most of whom have little or no familiarity whatsoever with trans, queer and feminist critiques of the gender binary. Borrowing on the increasingly popular hypothesis that sexual orientation is biologically-determined; the dominant discourse on gender variant children is now firmly anchored in sociobiology and medical pathology. For instance, in the *Globe* story, Nicole's doctor, Dr. Norman Spack, explained to Nicole's parents that: "the issue is a medical one and ... early intervention makes sense" (English). From this perspective, loving parents should recognize that transgender children are born with cross-gender identification. The compassionate and medically appropriate thing to do, according to Spack and other physicians who work with trans children, is to assist children in achieving the gender recognition they long for. This, they argue, is especially important given the potential consequences of not doing so: depression, isolation, suicide.

Indeed, *all* children deserve the gender recognition they long for, and they should have access to the tools—medical, therapeutic, aesthetic, political—to achieve this recognition. The problem lies, however, in the growing consensus that both gender fluidity and gender normativity are reflections of a child's innate and immutable constitution. The dominant discourse on childhood gender fluidity suggests that while there is a special band of children who are born with the gift of gender blending or cross identification, most children are, by contrast, gender normative. Experts on trans and "gender creative" children further suggest that it is the role of compassionate adults to allow children's genders to naturally unfold, while also looking for the emergent signs of cross-identification or gender fluidity. Of the utmost importance, we are told, is to let children *be who they are* (see Ehrensaft).

But what signs are we looking for as we look for children's gender-creative potential? *The Boston Globe*'s story about Nicole, for instance, offers the following evidence that Nicole (born Wyatt) was a girl: she liked Barbies, pink tutus, and beads (English). She also felt like a girl, and wanted to be a girl. The problem lies with the first part of this formulation, and not the second. All children need to be able to like pink, tutus, and beads without this signaling a fixed or core gender. But all children also need to be able to say, "I want you to understand that I am a girl (or boy, or girl-boy, or a robot)" and have that identification respected. Being a parent has clarified this distinction for me. Providing your child with gender self-determination means making no assumptions about whether colours, objects, moods, feelings, or skills have gendered meaning for your child. It means that when your child says, "I am a girl," you say, "Yes, Okay. Just today? Or all the time?" And you make it happen, depending on your child's answer. Your child's gender may change the next day, or your child may confidently identify as trans and ultimately want hormone therapy. In all cases, you are supportive. But you do not presume that a love of trucks or pink means *anything*, unless your child says it does. The narrative so frequently put forward by parents of trans kids—"I knew my child was transgender because s/he liked to play with xx toys and wear xx clothes"—does an injustice to all children, and to the project of gender self-determination more broadly. You only know your child is transgendered—or gendered at all—if they tell you so.

When male children, for instance, don't identify with their gender assignment, and when they have a passion for princesses, this does not mean they are *born* with a pink princess fetish and an intact girlhood, nor does it mean that they have a medical problem. This is because genders and their signifiers are invented to begin with, and children learn about the genders available to them and their culturally and historically specific meanings and implications, and then they choose—under considerable pressure and depending upon their capacity for rebellion—from among these possibilities. Children are born with body parts, including penises and vaginas, chromosomes, and hormones that have varied, complex, and frequently misunderstood effects. And that's all we know. That's simply all we know about the sex and gender of babies and young children. If we want to let children "be themselves," it would be hard to make a case for imposing or assuming anything other than this. When a child is born, we can note to ourselves, "well ... let's see ... I notice my child has a vagina," and then perhaps it would be wise to make queer/feminist plans to resist all the sexism and misogyny the world will likely direct at this vagina-possessing child. But calling this child a "girl" is already an imposition; this term presumes so much more than we know about the child. The moment we call this child a girl, we invite the world to see a pretty princess and to pretend that is who s/he always was. This point is something we teach in Women's Studies 101, but it's also something that even the best of feminists forget, and it's certainly something that very few dare to actually apply to their parenting.

The fact that reporting on trans children like Nicole has been far more sympathetic than reporting on Kathy Witterick and David Stocker's decision not to gender their child Storm is itself very telling. While it may be confusing and shocking for the general public to imagine raising a transgendered child, the story of trans children becomes relatable by making transgenderism analogous to medical disability. From this perspective, having a trans child is less than ideal, but it cannot be helped and there is a course of treatment to be pursued. In contrast, the idea that parents like Kathy and David would willfully choose to offer gender self-determination to their child provoked significantly more cultural anxiety, and Kathy and David's parenting came under vitriolic attack. Expert psychologists quoted by *ABC News* (James), *The Daily Mail* ("Are These the Most PC Parents in the World?"), and *The Toronto Star* (Poisson) described them as selfish, deceitful, impulsive, and manipulative radicals using their child to enact a damaging social experiment. They were subject to an investigation by Canada's child protection agency, and when Kathy and Storm were recognized in parks and supermarkets, strangers would scream angrily at them, "I know that's a boy!" or "I know that's a girl!" Kathy and David were shocked that it seemed no one could hear them saying that Storm will ultimately have a gender of some kind, but they (Storm's parents) are not going to be the ones who decide what it is.

Storm's parents were also surprised when advocates for trans and gender nonconforming children, like psychologist Diane Ehrensaft, publically declared their concern about ten-month-old Storm's mental health. Ehrensaft told *The Toronto Star*: "I believe this baby is not being given an opportunity to find their true gender self, based on what's inside them" (qtd. in Poisson). Following this lead, reporters accused Kathy and David of hiding "the truth" about Storm. As *The Daily Mail* reported, Storm's parents were keeping "whether this baby is a bruising boy or a blushing girl ... a secret" ("Are These the Most PC Parents in the World?"). And yet the infant Storm was not living in seclusion; those who wanted to know whether Storm was blushing or bruising—or any other aspect of Storm's *personality*—could have simply paid attention to Storm's ... personality! (to the extent that one-year-old infants possess them). Here, as is true of the gender binary more generally, genitals stood in for everything that adults wanted to know about Storm. For not revealing what they knew about Storm's genitals, Kathy and David were accused of hiding Storm's very selfhood. And indeed, this was far more threatening than a story about a child trapped in the wrong body, a child who—with the support of loving, heteronormative parents—can be fixed by a host of doctors.

GENDER SELF-DETERMINATION FOR *ALL* CHILDREN

When we apply the insights of queer and feminist theory to the work of raising children, we become invested in providing *all children*—not just those who "show the signs" of gender nonconformity—with the social, cultural, and political tools they can use to simultaneously work with and against the gender binary—a process I refer to as gender self-determination. Providing children with gender self-determination involves two efforts: 1) active cultivation of children's familiarity with and appreciation for genderqueer imagery, language, bodies, politics, and subculture; and 2) welcoming children's engagement with gender signifiers (gendered colours, toys, objects, images, feelings, and modes of relating) without "gender diagnosis," or the imposition of meaning about what children themselves are signifying—about their identities or their nature. Gender self-determination introduces children to the relational and culturally-embedded pleasures associated with gender play, without concretizing a gendered selfhood. It recognizes that neither children nor the world are "gender neutral." Nor are any of our genders "independent" from the cultures in which we are located; hence the term "gender independent"—a term gaining momentum among child advocates in Toronto—cannot quite capture the queer project. And moreover, it recognizes that no single child has a greater innate capacity for gender creativity or fluidity than another. All children have this potential, and therefore our project must not center on supporting special children, but on building a movement for all children's gender self-determination.

It is challenging to implement these ideas in our interactions with children because the world presents us with obstacles at every step. We have very few models for how to relate to children in genderqueer ways and the stakes and risks are extremely high. Someone may very well call child protective services and report that you are enacting a queer "social experiment" on your child—as if "experimenting" with liberationist parenting practices is something we should all agree to avoid.

As a parent engaged in my own queer parenting experiment, I offer here a modest set of guidelines:

1) *Don't refer to children as boys and girls*

Thankfully, many parents are starting to resist gender stereo-typing and allow for cross-gender exploration, often in the form of providing children with "dress up" clothes that allow for a broader range of play (male children in princess gowns, girls in Spiderman attire, etc.). But the vast majority of parents unthinkingly refer to their children as girls and boys, and they do this several times a day without considering the ways this makes sex/gender the central component of how kids think of themselves, understand their social group, and view themselves through their parents' eyes. Once children have been labeled girls or boys by the very adults they trust the most, they look to the social world for information about what these identities mean. To counteract the rigidity of the gender binary, often parents hope to redefine the meaning of boyhood or girlhood for their children. But even this liberal project sustains the gender binary by reinforcing the notion that humans come in two, biologically determined forms and by suggesting to children that they cannot escape their basic gender constitution.

I can think of only two reasons to refer to young children as if you know their gender identity: 1) You are doing some feminist/queer strategizing about how to combat the ways that children are diminished according to their *perceived* genders. 2) You need to talk about children's bodies for medical or other practical reasons, which isn't actually about gender anyway. If you need to talk about vaginas or penises, just do that.

Similarly, when talking about more than one child, don't call children "the boys" or "the girls." Don't use terms like "buddy" or "dude" or "precious" unless you use these words to describe all children, regardless of your perception of their gender, or unless you mix it up in a cool way (e.g., "princess dude") or you alternate (e.g., call your kid "dude" on Tuesday, "princess" on Wednesday).

2) *Queer your child*

Buy clothing or acquire hand-me-down clothing marketed to both boys and girls. If you have a child with a penis, do not refer to clothes marketed to girls, such as dresses, as "special" or "costumes" or "dress up;" this reinforces their strangeness or difference. Offering gender self-determination to children means trying not to impose on kids an adult relationship to gendered objects, even when those objects carry a lot of gendered baggage or associations for us (and are clearly are situated within structures of gender oppression). Until your child is old enough to create their own gendered style, aim for androgyny or alternate butch and femme aesthetics on different days. If your child has a vagina, the world expects long hair, so perhaps give them the experience of short hair before the weight of the gender binary comes crashing down in preschool. This, combined with pants, will mean that everyone will relate to your kid as a boy. You can go with that, you can mix it up, you can avoid the temptation to rescue your kid from what you might imagine is "misrecognition"—but you really have no idea what your kid's gender is until they tell you, so I say just calm down, breathe deep, and observe. What you *do* know is that all children will encounter the gender binary soon enough, so what you can offer in the meantime is an early familiarity with gender fluidity.

3) Don't diagnose your kid

Don't announce that despite your best feminist/queer efforts, your child is simply "a girly girl" or a "boy's boy." Do not make up a narrative about your child's gender, and do not believe that your child's own gendered narratives are fixed or have the same meaning to your child that they have to you. Let's say you have a child with a vagina who is obsessed with princesses. Avoid the temptation to say things like, "we've really tried to steer her away from princess stuff, but she's just a girly girl no matter what we do." If you have a child with a penis who turns paper towels into weapons at every turn, don't say, "gosh, I hate to admit it but I guess testosterone really *does* have all the effects they say it does!" This may shut down or misrecognize whatever queer or feminist meanings that could be present within princess play or paper towel aggression, and it also fails to recognize that your child's gender will evolve over time and may be stifled by any worrying and labeling on the part of nearby adults. Redirect kids away from violence and towards human connection, but don't make any of it about gender.

4) *Change the words in books targeted to young children*

Rarely do I read a book to my two-year-old child without changing any of the words. While reading, I frequently change "he" to "she," as the former is terribly overused in kids' books as a universal pronoun to describe all animals and most people. I also will use "he" on one page and "she" on the next page to describe the same character, because, well, some people identify as both male and female. I change man/woman and boy/girl to "person," "friend," "kid," "the narrator," "our protagonist," "the soccer player," etc. (e.g., we have a book that we call "Frosty the Snow Friend"). I change "girls' toys" to "toys marketed to girls." To introduce genderqueerness where there never is any, I sometimes refer to as "daddies" the people who appear to be mothers in a given story (I learned this from my child, who really likes to mix it up!). I know it seems stuffy to change the word "he" to a word like "protagonist" or to talk about marketing with kids, but I like the way it teaches kids that we default to gender when we really mean something far more specific or complex.

5) *When an important adult thinks they need to know your child's gender, ask why*

It's less popular these days for schools to gender segregate children or speak openly about children's gender differences than it once was, but it *is* common for schools to proudly talk about the importance of "gender balance" as a form of diversity (i.e., "at our preschool, we are attentive to having an equal number of girls and boys.") But we need to ask why this is important. To me it reveals that the school expects kids to have a clearly defined gender and that they think gender is revealing something important about who kids are. We need to push back on that idea. When I went to *Toys 'R' Us* and asked a salesperson where I could find a plastic pool and was met with the response, "for a boy or a girl?" that was obviously ludicrous. But far more insidious are all of the medical records and preschool applications we have encountered which require us to label our kid as either a boy or a girl, and present this question as if it's really fundamental to our child's well being. We've started asking, "do we really need to answer this question? And if so, why?" We're often bullied into answering it, but at the very least we have raised the question.

In sum, few parents have been as brave and committed to gender self-determination as Kathy and David, but we can all certainly move in this direction by being much more specific about how little we know, and how much we don't know, about children and gender. As a parent of a two-year-old with a penis, I can say that I just don't know *anything* yet about my child's desired *gender*. I know my kid likes parks, sushi, cookies, puzzles, books, cuddling, pretending to be asleep, and jokes about poop. My kid loves my partner and I. And I'm pretty positive none of this has anything to do with my child's body parts or future gender/s.

WORKS CITED

"Are These the Most PC Parents in the World?" *The Daily Mail* May 24, 2011. Web.

Ehrensaft, Diane. *Gender Born, Gender Made: Raising Healthy Gender-Nonconforming Children*. New York: The Experiment, 2011. Print.

English, Bella. "Led By the Child Who Simply Knew" *The Boston Globe*. December 2011. Web.

Green, Jesse. "S/He" *New York Magazine* May 2012. Web.

Poisson, Jayme. "Parents Keep Child's Gender Secret." *The Toronto Star* May 21, 2011 Web.

James, Susan Donaldson "Baby Storm Born Genderless is Bad Experiment, Says Experts." *ABC News* May 26, 2011. Web.

3.
The Boy in the Red Dress

SUSAN GOLDBERG

H E'S WEARING IT AGAIN today. You can't tell that right now as he trudges to kindergarten in the snow on this Tuesday morning, his hand in mine. Right now, he's a four-year-old boy, in black snowpants and a bright red ski jacket with the hood pulled up over his head. Right now, he's safe from the cold, safe from the street crossings, my hand at the ready to yank him back if he darts suddenly—or, more likely, wanders absentmindedly—into the path of an oncoming car.

But underneath that red ski jacket, those black snowpants, he's wearing it.

At his locker, I help him out of his coat, help him to navigate the straps of his snowpants, help him to hang them on the hook he can barely reach. Underneath his outerwear, he's wearing black fleece sweatpants, a blue hoodie, zipped up to the top. Hand in hand, we approach his teacher.

"So, we went to Value Village this weekend," I begin, smiling perhaps a little too brightly.

She smiles back, cocks her head at me.

"And Rowan picked out a dress," I continue. (*$7.99—a steal!*)

She raises an eyebrow. Nods her head slowly. "O-*kay...*"

"And he's wearing it today."

Underneath his hoodie, tucked into the hem of his sweatpants, is a dress—*the* dress. Peel back the layers and you'll see it: bright red cotton; long sleeves; a luminous white heart silkscreened on the centre of its chest. His chest. He wore it all weekend, slept in it, wore it to his babysitter's house on Monday, will not let us launder it. He has tucked the dress—or, more precisely, *I* have tucked the dress—into the hem of his sweatpants, ostensibly in order to put on his outerwear. I haven't helped him untuck it.

I explain to his teacher, as he has asked me to do, that he would like her to talk to the kids about how boys and girls can wear whatever colours, whatever clothes, they would like.

"Okay," she says again, eyebrow still raised, and he runs off to join his friends.

Out of his earshot, I tell her that he's got a change of clothing in his bag if he needs to change, if he becomes uncomfortable. I tell her that we—and by "we" I mean me and Rachel, who is Rowan's other mommy—told him that it's very likely that some of the kids might laugh at him or tell him the boys don't wear dresses, and that he's okay with that. My words tumble out: there's not much time before the bell, she's busy.

I tell her that we told him that if he needs any help, he can go to her. He can go to her, right?

"Okay," she says, for the third time. I can't get a read on her. She pauses, smiles: "This is a first."

A first. This isn't what I wanted to hear. What about, *No problem! Dress-wearing boys? A dime a dozen! I've seen it all—the kids love it!*

"Well," I stammer, "I guess I'm honoured to be your first." She doesn't smile at my joke, and the space between us grows even more awkward. "I guess I'll go now," I say.

I have put a shirt—a long-sleeved, red-and-blue striped shirt—in Rowan's backpack, just in case. Just in case, I tell him, he decides he'd be more comfortable in it and would like to change. I have shown him what I term a "trick": if he'd like to wear his dress privately, just for himself, he can tuck it into his sweatpants, zip up his hoodie over it. But he does not want to change, does not want to keep his dress private, covered up, and even as I suggest these things, hoping he goes for them, I feel cheapened.

I realize I'm shaking as I walk Rowan across the hall to the classroom where he will begin his day. His dress is still tucked into his waistband. He's still wearing his hoodie, and I fiddle with the zipper, inching it up just a bit. You can't tell, right now, what lies underneath.

"I love you," I tell him. "I'm proud of you. Have a wonderful day."

"Mom," he says, pulling at the zipper of his sweatshirt, "can I take this off?"

"Yes," I say, "if you want."

"No," he says after a moment. "I'll keep it on..."

"Okay," I say. "It's up to you."

And I kiss him goodbye and tell him I love him, leave him, turning back as I walk toward the school doors to watch him: a four-year-old boy whose black sweatpants and blue hooded sweatshirt still hide the heart he wears on his chest. He stands still as a current of children moves around him, one hand fingering the zipper on his sweatshirt. I can't quite tell whether I will feel worse if he keeps it on or takes it off.

I'm proud of him, yes.

But am I proud of me?

* * *

It began, as these things do, innocently enough. He'd been fascinated in recent months by the colour pink and we, his feminist, queer mommies, had indulged him: pink Crocs, pink pajamas, a pink polo shirt, pink trim on his winter boots. And then he said he wanted a dress. And we said sure, why not? We put on *Free to Be ... You and Me* (no, really, we did put on *Free to Be ... You and Me*) and went to the store on Saturday. We bought two dresses, the red one with the heart for Rowan, and a maroon velvet party dress with a sash for his younger brother, Isaac.

We also picked up some fairy wings: tulle netting stretched over wire frames with straps for children to hook their arms through. When we got home, they couldn't get their regular clothes off fast enough. We zipped up zippers and fastened buttons and tied sashes and guided little arms through fairy straps. As he descended the staircase, modelling his new outfit, Rowan had that look, the look that he gets when he's so pleased about something, pleased and proud: a shy, wide smile; eyes slightly downcast, as though to look directly at you may just be too much to bear.

I knew that look. I recognized it from my own baby pictures, from the shots of me that time my grandmother came to town and managed coax my toddler hair into two wispy ponytails, a feat that my own parents hadn't had the skills—or, perhaps, the patience—to accomplish. My father snapped the photos of me gazing, stupefied with joy, into the mirror; rolling one shoulder and then the other forward, cocking my head to either side.

So, yes, I know the joy. I know, intimately, the exuberance of something so right, so beautiful. What it means to look, finally, the way you've always wanted to look, when the clothes and hairstyle match your inner picture of yourself and you become a butterfly instead of a caterpillar. What you'd sacrifice for that feeling.

The exuberance was catching; it permeated the winter weekend. Rowan insisted that Rachel and I put on dresses, too, and so we did, her in a pink T-shirt and denim skirt and me—not so much a dress person these days, but flexible—in a black skirt and tank top with the Union Jack embroidered on it in sequins. On Sunday, the boys' godmothers, Judy and Jill, came over for brunch. Rowan phoned them in advance to tell them of the new dress code, and they (not so much dress people either, but flexible) showed up in dresses as well. It was a morning of compliments, an ongoing round of, "I like your dress, Mom! You look pretty!"

"Thanks! I like your dress, too!"

"Thanks! And what do you think of my wings?"

What did I think of their wings? I loved their wings. I loved their pleasure. I loved these two little boys twirling in their dresses, cuddling on the couch. "Who's my good little baby brother fairy?" Rowan crooned, over and over, to Isaac. "Who's my little Snow White? I love you, my pretty little princess."

Sunday afternoon, Rowan had a play date with school friend. When it became apparent that the dress wasn't coming off, my anxiety levels pricked up just a bit. I phoned the friend's house, got his mother on the line to give her the heads up. Because you just don't know, do you, right? You just can't necessarily drop your four-year-old son off at a new place, an unknown household, in a red dress with a heart on its chest.

"Oh, no problem," she said. "Keegan's wearing pink nail polish right now. We were just talking this morning about how boys and girls can both wear pink."

Keegan initially laughed when he saw what Rowan was wearing, and then didn't mention it again. His younger sister initially thought that Rowan was a girl, and then asked why he was wearing a dress. "Because," my son answered, "everyone in my house was wearing a dress today."

Good answer, I thought.

So, first there was home. Home is the centre, and then the circle widens, ripples on a pond: A friend's house. On Monday, the babysitter's home. Safe spaces, all.

And so, it began, as I said, as these things do, innocently enough. But how, I worried, would it end?

* * *

Let me be clear about something, just in case. For the record, I'm not worried that Rowan—that either of my sons—is gay. I'm not worried that either is transsexual or transgendered. I'm not worried about the prospect that one or both of my sons might get off by wearing girls' or women's clothing.

I will clarify further: when I say that I am "not worried," I do not mean that I don't believe my sons are or will turn out to be gay or trans. That's their business. What I mean is that if, in the event that they are gay, or trans, are unable to pin down neatly into an identifiable gender category, then I don't see this as a worrisome prospect.

Actually, let's make this absolutely crystal clear: if one or both of my children is gay, transsexual, transgender, I will not "still love them," or "love them anyway" or "love them in spite of." If one or both of my sons grows up to somehow queer the boundaries and binaries of sexual identity, gender, I will be thrilled. For them, for the world. I will be elated with the fierce kind of joy of the parent who watches her child discover and pursue his or her or hir passion. I will be as happy as that little girl staring at her pigtailed self in that mirror.

That's what I tell myself.

But in the hallway of my son's elementary school, the circle has widened beyond the point where I can guarantee his safety. Here, he's one of 800 kids, the eldest of whom are bona fide teenagers. Here, I cannot follow him around like a one-woman PR firm, putting a positive, protective spin on his outfit. Here, I don't dictate the social codes, cannot pre-screen each interaction to ensure that no one taunts him, baits him, spits on him, pisses in his locker, beats him up.

And while I know that junior kindergarten is generally a pretty safe space, that my son's school is generally a pretty safe space, my mind keeps flashing to the spate of suicides by queer teens, by those perceived to be queer. I think of fourteen-year-old Lawrence King, wearing high heels and makeup to his California junior high school, shot to death by a classmate in February 2008. I think of the "It Gets Better" project, and I don't want my kids to know that it could get worse, much worse. And yet, I don't want him to hide his joy, to spurn the bright red centre of his self. I think of Shiloh Jolie-Pitt and Constance getting to take her girlfriend to the prom and of how much I am rooting for that girl in her suit and that boy—this boy—in his dress.

But that morning in that elementary school hallway, I desperately want that girl, that boy, to be someone else's kid.

* * *

So. Home, a friend's house, the babysitter's, the school. And now music class.

I'm always uncomfortable in music class: something about the vehement wholesomeness of it turns my stomach, and yet we signed Rowan up as a baby and he loves it, and so we keep coming back, hoping to make good on the promise that square-dancing with your baby in the basement of a strip-mall music studio will ensure his acceptance into Harvard. The studio's owner is an evangelical Christian, always incredibly welcoming of our family, of my kids, but in my head her faith looms large, makes me wonder what she really thinks. My doubts extend to the other families in the class: what do they think of me, my family?

I don't realize until Rowan is unzipping his coat that he has worn his dress to music class. I'm momentarily thrown, but there's no going back. And before I can fret too much about what comments or judgments my son's outfit might incur, another kid, Matty, bounces in. Wearing pajamas. His mother rolls her eyes, settles down with her book.

And then James appears. James, whose father is a mountain

of a man, huge and solid; his five-year-old son literally climbs him, perches on the top of his enormous, bald head, lies across his shoulders as though they are a bed. James's father appears uncomfortable in music class, unsure of what to do in the midst of all the bell-ringing and tambourine-tapping and yodelling and nursery rhymes. I have heard James's mom talking about her husband, about how he doesn't quite get this whole music thing. "It's a little bit too girly for him," she once said, laughing.

James is resplendent in a blue and green stripy sweater that is on not only inside-out but also backwards. The tag—his name written on it in Sharpie—juts out jauntily just beneath his clavicle.

But James's sweater is the least of it. James also boasts two violently black eyes. James has an egg-sized, green/blue bruise on his forehead. James looks like someone beat him, bad. "He was swinging on the door between the bed and a dresser," says his father, quickly, desperately, by way of hello; rushing to get the words out, there's not much time: "and he slammed his face into the hardwood floor."

I realize in that moment James's father has probably spent the past week cringing anytime anyone has looked at his son, worried that passersby might call Children's Aid. James's father is worried sick that people will think that he is a monster. James's father saw his son fly through the air and land, face first and bloodied, on an unforgiving surface.

James's father, I realize, doesn't give a rat's ass about my son's dress with a red heart on the centre of his chest.

* * *

My kid, though—both my kids—persist in wearing their dresses out in public. When I am with them, I begin to adopt the persona of a mama lion: relaxed but watchful, protective. I'm on the lookout for snickers, questions. I exude—at least I hope I exude—a "don't mess with me or my kids" attitude that belies my nervousness.

We widen the circle. And as we do, my fears, my watchfulness, begin to recede. Sometimes, as it tends to be with most things child-related, it feels like we're just part of the larger demographic. We go to dinner at a friend's house, and their five-year-old son, also the child of two moms, greets us at the door in his dress. Isaac wears his purple velvet dress to Hebrew school; we arrive to find his classmate, three-year-old Simon, in an *Alice in Wonderland* outfit. "Didn't you get the memo?" I ask the parents of the third three-year-old boy in the class. They look at me blankly.

"Shea likes to wear dresses," my stepbrother remarks offhandedly about his own three-year-old son, as we watch our collective offspring fling themselves off the tops of the bunk bed. "He looks pretty good in them."

"Why is Rowan wearing a dress?" It's the kids who ask these questions, usually to their parents, sometimes to me, very occasionally directly to him. "Because I want to," is invariably his answer. "Because he wants to," is mine, invariably, too. "Because boys can wear dresses if they want to" is the answer the other parents usually give, occasionally amended with, "and I think he looks very handsome today."

"Oh, my nephew wore a dress every day for two years," says my friend Mel. "And the kids would laugh at him sometimes and he would just say, 'I don't care. I love my dress.' It was awesome."

"Well, *hello* ladies," the waitress at the Scandinavian Home Restaurant says to us as she lays down cutlery and napkins, fills our water glasses. "And don't you look lovely today." There's not a trace of anything but kindness in her voice. And my sons smile and smooth their skirts. At soccer, my friends Sue and Derek's toddler son is wearing his yellow skirt again; their biggest problem is that he refuses to wear any sort of underwear at all underneath it.

"I love your dress!" exclaims our friend's eleven-year-old son, when he runs into Isaac at the farmers market. "I used to wear dresses all the time."

Boys in dresses? A dime a dozen. Nothing new.

Right?

Inasmuch as I am engaged in a process of crossing gender boundaries, I can't help but notice that it's the little boys who seem most genuinely curious, slightly confused, mostly benign. More often than not it's the girls who giggle, who point out the rules and our apparent flaunting of them. "But why?" One girl in his class asks me this almost daily, every time she sees me: "Why does he wear a dress? Why does he have pink boots?" I smile at her between gritted teeth: "The same reason you do: he likes them."

"Both boys and girls love to play dress-up and they often dress as the opposite gender, especially during the preschool years," says an article in I stumble across a parenting magazine that we subscribed to years ago and that we still can't get rid of. "A child learns about gender roles by identifying with important people in his life, and will typically settle into behaviours and preferences that match his biological sex by about age six. If he says he wants to be a girl, avoids participation in stereotypically 'boy' activities or expresses negative feelings about his sexual anatomy, you should consult a qualified children's mental health practitioner" (Sabbagh).

No, I think, YOU *should consult a qualified children's mental health practitioner.*

But who am I talking to in my head? Certainly not my kids, stable and happy in their sartorial choices. Whose thinking warrants scrutiny? What about the educators trying to quash gay-straight alliances, who insist that girls must wear dresses and boys tuxedos to the prom? Certainly, it's the world at large—the publishers of children's books, the media, the government, the churches and the hospitals and the mental health practitioners, the toy and clothing designers—who need to rethink these things, to widen the circles of safety and joy that surround our collective children and how they present themselves in this world.

But what about me? What about my own fears, my clenched fists; what about me, zipping up the zipper on my kid's hoodie, hiding his heart? What about my constant vigilance, my focus on the one thing that might hurt him, instead of the dozens of examples of kindness my community has shown to me, to my family, my sons? What do I teach them when I let my fear become so palpable that it threatens to override their beauty? What's the right balance between protecting them and hurting them?

I think of Rowan, now seven and a half, strong and fast and passionate about soccer and Pokémon, hair halfway down his back, vehement in his opinions and in his confidence in his abilities. I think of him a month or so ago at the public swimming pool, getting up the courage to jump off the diving board for the first time. He climbs the ladder, turns back. Climbs it again, gets all the way to the edge of the board and hesitates. Of course, he could drown. He could plummet down and swallow water and hurt himself, never come up again. Of course he could. I watch him, hands clenched, holding my breath waiting, waiting, hoping—and then he is off, flying through the air, landing with a splash and going under. I watch him resurface, grinning, looking around wildly for me and smiling. "I did it!" he calls, and I nod and clap, thrilled. Around him, the water ripples out in concentric circles, ever widening, ever-growing, and I am breathless, gleeful, watching him swim to the ladder for another go. The water streams over his heaving chest and if you look closely you'd swear you could see it, just underneath the skin: the beating of his beautiful, luminous, heart.

WORKS CITED

Sabbagh, Ruwa. "Playing Dress-up: Some Pointers on How to Delicately Handle the Situation." *Today's Parent* November 2009. Web. Accessed June 7, 2012.

4.
Transgender Men's Self-Representations of Bearing Children Post-Transition

DAMIEN W. RIGGS

SINCE REPORTS OF THOMAS BEATIE'S PREGNANCY appeared in the media in 2008, the visibility of transgender men having children post-transition has increased considerably. Whilst this visibility, it may be argued, have attracted negative attention to transgender men who choose to bear a child (and transgender men more broadly), it may also be argued that representations of transgender men bearing children has usefully drawn attention to the complex negotiations that transgender men undertake in having children. At the heart of these negotiations lies what is often framed as a competition between transgender men's masculinity, and their undertaking of a role historically undertaken by people who identify as women (i.e., child bearing). Yet what is repeatedly demonstrated in transgender men's own self-representations of their pregnancies post-transition, is that they are very much men, even if their masculinity is placed in question by a society that equates child bearing with women.

The present chapter takes transgender men's self-representations as its starting place in seeking to elabourate how such men reconcile their masculinity with child bearing. In so doing, the chapter seeks to bring the social scientific literature about transgender men who bear children post-transition together with the public self-representations of such men in order to begin the work of mapping out the unique experiences of men who undertake a pregnancy. Whilst transgender men become parents in a multitude of ways (i.e., when still living as their natally-assigned sex, through their partners bearing children, and through forms of non-genetically related kinship such as adoption), it is argued here that, given the non-normative account of masculinity that is produced by transgender men who bear children, this specific mode of family formation requires closer attention. In the following sections the chapter first outlines the two main challenges expressed by transgender men who bear children in previous social scientific research, before going on to explore how transgender men who bear children account for their masculinity and pregnancies to the media. Exploring public representations of men who undertake a pregnancy are important for the ways in which they both highlight and discount the alleged dissonance that is thought to exist in the case of transgender men who bear children, as Paisley Currah outlines so well:

> Some bodies are modified through hormones, various types of gender reassignment surgeries, or both, to produce bodies culturally commensurate with gender identities. In those cases, the perceived incongruence comes only from knowing the *history* of that individual's body. Other bodies, however, have unexpected configurations in their particular *geographies*—for example, breasts with penises for some, male chests with vaginas for others—that produce a dissonance. (This dissonance, to be clear, belongs not to the trans body but to those gazers who have conventional gender expectations.) (331)

As Currah suggests, many transgender people are able to live their lives without other people knowing their transgender status. Transgender men who bear children, by contrast, are *a priori* treated as bodies requiring an explanation. That such men are faced with an injunction to explain their masculine embodiment is, as Currah so rightly points out, very much a product of cisgender bodily norms.

Yet understanding how transgender men account for their embodied experiences is nonetheless important for offering guidance to those who engage with transgender men who bear children, in addition to recognizing the experiences of transgender men themselves.

PREVIOUS RESEARCH

There has to date been very little research undertaken with transgender men who bear children post-transition. This may be for any number of reasons, but likely includes 1) the relative recency of public awareness about transgender men bearing children (and this includes awareness amongst transgender men that this is an option), 2) the willingness (or otherwise) of transgender men to speak publically about their pregnancies, and 3) the relative infancy of non-pathologising transgender studies. The research that does exist suggests two main areas where transgender men who bear children must negotiate issues associated with their embodied masculinity, as outlined below.

Pregnancy

Pregnancy brings with it for transgender men two challenges that are primarily the product of the normative assumption that only women carry children. The first of these relates to how men understand themselves as men whilst they are pregnant. Previous research suggests that some transgender men reconcile their pregnancies through the notion of simply being a 'host' for the child. Thus as one participant in Sam Dylan More's research suggested: "I didn't regard the unborn child as a part of my person, rather as a guest" (Matt qtd. in More 321). Making a distinction between the unborn child and themselves, it would appear, allows some transgender men to maintain a line between the role their body is playing, and their identity as a man.

The second challenge faced by transgender men in terms of carrying a child is in regards to having to interact with doctors, as clearly illustrated in the following example taken from More's research:

> Having to be examined pelvicly repulsed me to an exaggerated degree, I thought. Sitting in the docs office who delivered me, and my mom, and Zac was also humiliating in an (en)gendered way: that space was woman's space and fundamentally at the surface of my skin I didn't fit in. (Del qtd. in More 322)

Here Del speaks of how engaging with doctors forcibly brought him back into his own body, one normatively marked by the medical profession and society more broadly as female by the fact of his pregnancy.

Maura Ryan's research with transgender men who bear children post-transition, however, suggests that "[Men who had born a child] conceptualized themselves as men who had the unique opportunity to become pregnant" (145). Rhetorically this type of conceptualization constructs transgender men who bear children as *unique men,* rather than as men with female bodies. This, it could be argued, provides an important counter to the challenges experienced by men in the previous two examples.

Breastfeeding

Once transgender men have given birth, a subsequent challenge identified in previous research is breastfeeding. Interestingly, previous research suggests that transgender men adopt a pragmatic or utilitarian approach to breastfeeding, where breastfeeding is seen as serving a purpose (and thus that breasts have some use). Participants in Henry Rubin's research suggested that, for them, breastfeeding was the only time in which their breasts did not seem like an unwanted part of their body (as they were serving a purpose), a point also made by one of More's participants:

> When I was alone I had no problems breastfeeding, it was very natural, animal-like. But when company was present they related to me as female, even when they didn't say it. It was extremely uncomfortable. (Matt qtd. in More 325)

As Matt suggests, breastfeeding was fine unless it involved company, in which case, like the previous example from Del, Matt is forced back into a body that is treated as female, rather than simply a unique male body. Yet despite the challenge presented by other people's views of their bodies, More suggests that in general her participants, when viewing breastfeeding as a 'technical' or functional aspect of their embodiment, could accept it as a "'gender-neutral' activity which had been chosen out of anatomical necessity" (326).

TRANSGENDER MEN'S SELF-REPRESENTATIONS

This section reports on five instances where transgender men have spoken publically about their experiences of pregnancy. These instances were identified through a Google search for the key terms 'transgender pregnancy', 'trans man parent', 'transgender parenting', and 'trans father'. It is of course recognized that, as with any media report, only particular questions are likely to have been asked, and the framing of media reports typically aims to generate reader interest through sensationalism. Nonetheless, in the documentaries, news reports, and blogs examined here, it can be argued that much of what appears are transgender men's own accounts of their pregnancies, accounts that very much echo what is found in previous research.

In terms of carrying a child, some of the self-representations identified repeated the idea that men who carry children are simply 'hosts':

> I've never felt like his mother. I breastfed for eleven, almost twelve months of his first year, but as far as a mother I don't feel like it, I just feel like wow, guys can have babies. I'm like, I guess, an incubator or something. (Terry qtd. in Rosskam)

> It really didn't occur to me that [the pregnancy] was actually happening to me. It was me looking at this another person being pregnant. It was like handling it by remote control from some control room somewhere. (Jarek qtd. in Rosskam)

Whilst it could be argued that in some instances such distancing rhetoric may place some transgender men at risk for not addressing pregnancy-related issues (i.e., by ignoring physiological responses), this did not appear in any of the self-representations examined. Rather, the men appeared to use distancing techniques to cordon off certain aspects of the pregnancy from their identity as men. In other words, they very much considered themselves as responsible for the pregnancy, yet the pregnancy was not their own *per se*.

In terms of breastfeeding, one of the self-representations identified appeared in a blog written by Trevor MacDonald, who writes explicitly as a transgender man who breastfed the child he carried, despite having had a mastectomy:

> The word "breastfeeding" doesn't bother me. Both men and women have breast tissue and can, unfortunately, get breast cancer. We all have nipples and breasts, to a certain extent. Furthermore, breastfeeding is not about sex—it is about feeding a baby. It doesn't make me feel feminine or female to feed Jacob. I do also use the term nursing frequently though. (FAQ)

Here MacDonald clearly orientates to an account of breast-feeding premised upon utility: that breastfeeding doesn't compromise his masculinity, as 'breasts' are not gender specific, and as he argues more broadly throughout the blog, he believes breastfeeding is important for babies and thus it was something that had to be done.

As was the case with previous research, some men identified challenges that arose from engaging with clinics in their journey:

> It is truly magical to watch what happens when a trans person produces an [Ontario Heath Insurance Policy] card at any medical visit. The 'F' on the card miraculously erases any existing effects of testosterone, top surgery, dress, and name choice. According to the Government of Ontario, I *was* a woman. The receptionist at the intake desk simply following the silent directive printed on my OHIP card, and told me "Miss, there is a long wait today so go with the technician to get changed and then have a seat with the other women at the end of the hall." (Ware 69)

This example highlights the fact that regardless of transgender men's own negotiations of masculinity in the context of pregnancy, they must also contend with how other people treat them (and indeed misgender them). This point is of particular note given that the issue raised by Syrus Ware is not necessarily transphobia *per se* (though this is not to say that transgender men who bear children do not encounter explicit transphobia from health care professionals), but rather that the mundane imposition of gender norms upon transgender men can exacerbate the challenges they already face in negotiating pregnancy (Riggs).

Despite the challenges of negotiating public perceptions of their pregnancies, a recurrent theme in the self-representations examined here was a sense that pregnancy allowed transgender men to view their bodies as having a purpose, as Scott Moore elabourates:

> I really do think that I was lucky to be able to carry Miles. I think, for the longest time my body, and being transgendered, was such a negative thing for me, and made me so uncomfortable. And even though the process of being pregnant and giving birth isn't the most comfortable thing, it made me appreciate what I have more, and realize that even though it's not the ideal of what I'd like to be, it's still beautiful. (Moore and Moore).

Echoing a point made by Ryan in previous research, then, Moore's account of his pregnancy emphasizes that the unique experience of being a pregnant man in some ways counteracts the marginalizing and for many people distressing experience of living in a body that does not match with their identity. A similar claim was made by two participants in the documentary *TransParent*, who suggest "That time during the pregnancy was the only time, absolutely the only time I felt right being in a female body" (Alex qtd. in Rosskam) and "That's the only time in my whole life I've felt right in my body. When I was pregnant and nursing for almost nine months, my body was doing what it was supposed to be doing, it was doing it by itself, and it felt absolutely right" (Joey qtd. in Rosskam). This logic of pregnancy paradoxically contributing to, rather than undermining, a stable transmasculine identity, is highlighted in the following and final quote from Thomas Beatie:

> How does it feel to be a pregnant man? Incredible. Despite the fact that my belly is growing with a new life inside me,

I am stable and confident being the man that I am. In a technical sense I see myself as my own surrogate, though my gender identity as male is constant.

What it appears pregnancy does for some transgender men, then, is rather than making them feel *less* like men, instead vindicates for them that they *are* men precisely because they don't feel like a woman carrying a child.

CONCLUSION

Of course the final point made in the above analysis begs the question of whether transgender men's accounts of pregnancy are always already reliant upon a normative binary of what a woman is and what a man is, and the role that each is expected to play. Judith Halberstam summarizes this well in saying:

> Beatie, as many of the stories about him confirm, was a beauty pageant participant in his early years in Hawaii, and so the spotlight is not an uncomfortable place for him to find himself. He dealt well with the glare of the cameras in general, but, rather than promoting a queer narrative about difference and gender shifts, his story ultimately came to rest upon an all too familiar narrative of humanity and universality—it is universal to want a child, it is only human to want to give birth. The Beaties just wanted, in other words, what supposedly everyone else wants—the good life, reproductive potential, a bit of extra cash, and some publicity to boot. Beatie's very public pregnancy certainly afforded him and his family a nice slice of fame and fortune, but we would be very mistaken if we imagined that any political agenda had been advanced by the smiling, comforting image of the male Madonna, cradling his full belly and assuring U.S. viewers that everything is still in its right place. (78)

At the same time, however, this chapter highlights the fact that it is indeed possible for pregnancy to be detached from its normative relationship to particular embodied identities (i.e., female), and to instead reconceptualize pregnancy as a role that can be fulfilled by any embodied identity (albeit one that occupies a body capable of bearing a child). What the men reported here are negotiating, then, is a script for being a father in a society that does not view fathers as child bearers, and moreover that labels particular behaviours as maternal (i.e., child bearing, breastfeeding) and others as paternal (i.e., everything that the maternal is not).

As such, the transgender men whose self-representations appear in this chapter engage with the central question addressed by Andrea Doucet in her book-length study on whether or not men who are primary parents mother or indeed become mothers. Whilst Doucet's research focused on cisgendered men, the findings are arguably applicable to transgender men as well, namely that given all of the attributions made about the category 'mother' (which is tightly regulated in relation to gender norms), men (cisgendered or transgendered) cannot be mothers. That some men do bear children, then, is a physiological fact. But we can impute nothing from this fact about the identity of such men (i.e., that they are not men).

Rather, the experiences of transgender men reminds us that biology and identity are two separate issues, and that supporting and recognizing transgender men who carry children requires an approach that engages both with the body itself (i.e., the specific issues that pregnant bodies experience), but which does so in conjunction with an engagement with the person who occupies the body (i.e., in this case a man). This requires recognition of the fact that health care professionals must acknowledge how gender norms shape individual health care needs, and that whilst there may be some similarities between pregnant men and pregnant women (i.e., carrying a child), there will also be vast differences according both to the individual's experience of their gendered body, as well as the differences in their physiology at a hormonal, physical and psychological level. Engaging with trans men who bear children, then, requires a specific approach that recognizes such men *as men,* and does not default to norms for pregnancy defined historically by the experiences of women.

WORKS CITED

Beatie, Thomas. "Labour of Love." *Advocate* April 3, 2008. Print.

Currah, Paisley. "Expecting Bodies: The Pregnant Man and Transgender Exclusion." *Women's Studies Quarterly* 36 (2008): 330-336. Print.

Doucet, Andrea. *Do Men Mother?* Toronto: University of Toronto Press. Print.

Halberstam, Judith. "The Pregnant Man." *The Velvet Light Trap* 65 (2010): 77-78. Print.

MacDonald, Trevor. *Milk Junkies blog.* Web. Accessed: November 6, 2012.

Moore, Tom and Scott Moore. "My Pregnant Dad." *20/20* Interview. August 25 (2011).

More, Sam Dylan. "The Pregnant Man—An Oxymoron?" *Journal of Gender Studies* 7 (1998): 319-328. Print.

Riggs, Damien. "What Makes a Man? Thomas Beatie, Embodiment, and 'Mundane Transphobia'." *Feminism and Psychology* (in-press).

Rosskam, Jules, dir. *TransParent.* Documentary, 2005.

Rubin, Henry. *Self-Made Men: Identity and Embodiment Among Transsexual Men.* Nashville: Vanderbilt University Press, 2003. Print.

Ryan, Maura. "Beyond Thomas Beatie: Trans Men and the New Parenthood." *Who's Your Daddy? And Other Writings on Queer Parenting.* Ed. Rachel Epstein. Toronto: Sumach Press, 2009. 139-150. Print.

Ware, Syrus Marcus. "Boldly Going Where Few Men Have Gone Before: One Trans Man's Experience." *Who's Your Daddy? And Other Writings on Queer Parenting.* Ed. Rachel Epstein. Toronto.

5.
Trapped in the Wrong Body
and Life Uncharted

Anticipation and Identity Within Narratives of Parenting Transgender/Gender Non-conforming Children

JESSICA ANN VOORIS

A FAMILY IN TORONTO made the news in May 2011 when they declared that they were not going to reveal the sex of their baby, in order to free him/her from the gendered expectations of those around him/her. The story was first reported by *The Toronto Star*, "Parents Keep Baby's Gender a Secret" (Poisson 2011a) but soon spread around the world and garnered such headlines as, "Canadian Mother Raising 'Genderless' Baby, Storm, Defends Her Family's Decision" (Davis). Kathy Witterick and David Stocker wrote a letter to friends and family explaining their choice, "We've decided not to share Storm's sex for now—a tribute to freedom and choice in place of limitation, a stand up to what the world could become in Storm's lifetime (a more progressive place?...)" (Poisson 2011a). The news coverage of their decision ignited a firestorm in the blogosphere and in the comment sections of the articles, with many people condemning Witterick and Stocker, arguing that the baby will grow up confused (Poisson 2011b). There were also numerous comments against some of the other parenting decisions Witterick and Stocker have made, such as allowing their children to choose their own clothes and hairstyles, and choosing to "unschool" their children.[1] While they are a conventional family in other ways—white, heterosexual, married, middle-class—these noted parenting practices are viewed alongside the decision around their baby's gender as evidence of poor parenting. In both Witterick and Stocker's decision making, as well as in the critiques of their choices, there is an appeal to the future possibilities of this child's life, either one in which the world will become a more progressive place, or one where the individual child is damaged by the choices his/her parents have made.

In this chapter I argue that anticipation work, in which parents are preparing for the best possible outcome in terms of their children's well being and happiness, permeates narratives of parenting transgender/gender non-conforming/queer children. Sexuality and gender identity are usually attached to an adult subject, and the idea of a "gay child" during the twentieth century was from the perspective of an adult looking backwards (Stockton). This belief is changing however, and as more children, parents, and professionals are (self) identifying and/or naming children as gay and transgender, we see how their identities and bodies are informed by ideas around gender and sexuality. I use the idea of anticipation and a critique of identity politics to examine the narratives created within the media and through parents' blogs about children's gender identities, potential sexualities, and sexed bodies. Within these narratives an emphasis is placed on how children identify with a particular gender identity or expression from a young age, the strength of their identification with the norms of their chosen gender, and the extreme distress that influenced their parents' decisions around letting children express themselves. I argue that in each of these narratives about children's bodies and identities we see anticipation work, which reflects particular understandings of the past to make sense of the present, and involves preparing for the future, while grappling with the ambiguity of future identities and possibilities (Adams, Murphy and Clarke).

The story about baby Storm was just one in a number of stories in 2011 addressing the question of children's gender identity and expression. There were also news stories about princess boys (Dube) and transgender children (Park; Ling) as well as controversy over a photo in *J.Crew* of a mother painting her son's toenails pink (Donaldson James). This media attention has only intensified in 2012, with news articles in *The Washington Post* (Dvorak), *LA Times* (Gorman), and *New York Magazine* (Green) on families with transgender children, as well as articles examining the phenomenon of boys wearing dresses (Padawer). Each of these have looked at families who are raising their children in a way that counters societal norms about the way boys and girls are supposed to act, and instead follow the children's lead on how they want to express their gender. A recent story out of Germany shows a father taking it one step further, changing his own behaviour and wearing a skirt in support of his son's preference for skirts (Pickert). The last two years have also seen an increase in the number of blogs written by parents (mostly mothers) of transgender, gender-nonconforming, and gay children chronicling their parenting experiences, which often reflect more complicated and nuanced realities than shown within the media.

While stories around gender non-conformity, and transsexualism in particular, have long been of interest to the public, as pointed out by Joanne Meyerowitz in *How Sex Changed: A History of Transsexuality in the United States,* these news reports point to increased awareness and attention to gender non-conformity in *children* and the need to either correct the behaviour of these children or support them in their choices. While these articles and blogs receive many positive comments about the parents' support of their children, there is also backlash, and societal pressure to make these children conform to what are seen as proper gender roles. For instance, in February 2012, a preacher in South Carolina advocated that parents punch a boy who shows effeminate behaviour in an effort to teach him to act like a man, although he later retracted, saying it was just a joke (Hooper; Murdoch; Harris). Considering the violence that many children, youth and adults face for defying gender norms, as well as the high risk of suicide and self-harm for LGBTQ[2]-identified youth, it is important to have information that helps us better understand trans/queer narratives and gendered parenting practices.

Much of the research on gender non-conformity, or gender variance, in children has focused on femininity in boys. In the 1950s and 1960s, psychoanalysts began paying increased attention to the phenomenon of feminine boys, and in particular developed frameworks for preventing gender non-conforming behaviour in order to prevent adult outcomes such as homosexuality, transsexuality, and transvestitism (Bryant 2006). While girls were not completely ignored in this research and it was noted that tomboys were at risk of becoming lesbians, boys received far more attention, and critics have theorized that this is because of general anxieties around masculinity, as well as the undervaluing of femininity (Bryant 2006). Karl Bryant argues that "Given that gender variant children have multiple possible trajectories (and trajectories for individual young children are hard to predict), one of the goals across the 50 years of work on gender variant children, sometimes explicit but more often tacit, has been an attempt at encouraging some outcomes and discouraging others. One symptomatic result of the goal has been an implied hierarchy of preferred, acceptable, and unacceptable outcomes concerning sexual orientation and gender identity" (2008: 465). Even as transgender and gay children gain acceptance, there is still a favoring of particular narratives over others, and the management of particular futures over more ambiguous ones.

The understanding of homosexuality and transgender as separate categories is historically contextualized, and is due to contemporary (twentieth century) understandings of "gender" and "sexuality" as being ontologically and essentially different (Valentine; Meyerowitz. See also Foucault and D'Emilio). As Meyerowitz writes, many of those who previously were included in the general category "invert" began "sorting themselves out. In each group, those who sought respectability hoped to avoid the label of freak or status of outcast" (184). Transsexuals tried to distance themselves from homosexuality and "queers" and, in turn, gay and lesbians emphasized 'normal' gender identities. The term transgender itself arose in the 1970s as a term for those who identified between transsexual and transvestite, but has become known as a collective term to describe a variety of (adult) identifications: cross-dressers, female impersonators, trans women and trans men who have transitioned from their gender assigned at birth, butch lesbians, and the list goes on.[3] In the case of children "Transgender" indicates a child who identifies as the opposite gender, while a variety of other labels, such as gender-non-conforming, gender-variant, gender-creative, tomboy, tomgirl, pink boys, and princess boy are used to describe those who express their gender differently.[4]

MEDIA REPRESENTATIONS:
GENDERED BEHAVIOUR AND TRAPPED IN THE WRONG BODY

The first TV special on transgender children was ABC's *20/20* "My

Secret Self: A Story of Transgender Children," which aired in 2007, follows the stories of three individuals and their families: six-year-old Jazz and ten-year-old Riley who are trans girls, and Jeremy, a sixteen-year old trans boy.[5] Since then, transgender children have been seen on *The Tyra Show, Dr. Oz, Anderson Cooper's 360,* and *Our America with Lisa Ling.* In general these shows are sympathetic in their portrayals, and serve to educate viewers about trans children. Parents provide evidence of their children's interest in particular clothing and toys and the documentaries show the children's rooms as being appropriately masculine or feminine to match their gender identity. A lot of attention is given to the fact that the gender non-conforming behaviour happens before it is typically thought that children have a concept of gender. For example, Jazz, from the original ABC *20/20* special is said to have unsnapped her onesies to make a dress at the age of eighteen months. Attention is also given to scenes of the children getting dressed, putting on make-up (girls) and having their hair cut (boys).

While educating viewers that sex is different from gender identity, in many ways these children's stories reify the idea of gender norms regardless of biological anatomy; girls like pink and wear dresses and boys like sports and have short hair. Jane Ward makes a similar point in her chapter in this anthology to what I am outlining here that these preferences are seen as proof for an innate gender, ignoring the social, historical and cultural meanings attached to particular clothes, hair styles and toys. Recognition of children's gender identity and autonomy is important, particularly given the fact that gender and sexuality are usually understood to be adult subjectivities. I agree with Jane Ward's argument that gender self-determination should be granted to all children, not just "gender non-conforming" children.

The focus on gender performance in the TV documentaries functions as a way of proving identity and also showing the ways in which the past is used to understand the present and to plan the future. The narrative of the documentaries tacks back and forth from past to present, as before and after photos are shown, with emphasis placed on old names being changed to new ones, and stories of children's past distress and present happiness. Here we see how the past informs the present, and the idea of a future (Adams, Murphy, Clarke).

In these documentaries, discussions center on each individual family's journey and experience, without situating them within larger historical narratives of transgendered lives and societal pressures around gender conformity. Emily Manual argues that transgender children are treated more sympathetically than adult trans people because they are seen as innocent, natural, and non-sexual, yet "[w]hile it's wonderful to see trans children treated as actual living breathing human beings, and more positive representations will definitely help those children gain access to blockers and hormones, what happens when they grow up?" Furthermore, what about the raced and classed inequalities that are unaddressed in these documentaries which focus mostly on white, middle-class families? It is important to think about the future not only in terms of individual children's lives but also (future) conceptualizations of broader social equality.

Along with gendered behaviour, the documentaries focus on children's bodies, and on some of the medical and psychological issues that they are dealing with. This includes examination of past traumas, as well as future possibilities around hormones and surgery. When facing opposition to their identities and having been told that their body/biology is their identity, these children often react in extreme ways with self-mutilation and/or suicidal ideation. Hailey's mother, interviewed by Lisa Ling for the "Our America" special, describes how her daughter ran into a busy street, and afterwards said she was trying to die. On *20/20* and "I Am Jazz," Jazz's mother recounts Jazz explaining that she wished that she no longer existed because then she would not be dealing with her pain, and her mommy wouldn't be sad either. In the 2011 *20/20* special "Boys will be Girls," Dr. Joanne Olsen from the Children's Hospital in L.A., points out the necessity for parents to support their children and to recognize that gender non-conformity looks different for everyone. She argues "there are some kids who absolutely cannot function unless they socially transition" and asks parents "would you rather have a dead son than an alive daughter" because "these kids have a suicidal rate that is astronomical."

It seems that in order for these children's requests to be met, justified and explained, their stories must include the extreme. While this may reflect their particular realities, I argue that emphasizing the extreme also makes invisible those children who do not feel an urgent need to change their bodies. Furthermore, it indicates that children's ability to make choices about their gender identity is only justified by the threat of a death. Meyerowitz describes the way that increasing information and press about transsexuals in the second half of the twentieth century gave people the language to describe their desires, and let them know that they were not alone. However, questions around surgery and medical attention were often fraught with issues of control and authority. Trans people learned to tell the stories that the doctors wanted to hear, making sure they fit diagnostic categories, presenting a respectable demeanour and proper femininity or masculinity, and also emphasizing the urgency of the surgery by discussing suicide.

Media representations use the frameworks of "trapped in the wrong body" and "birth defect" to understand these children's experiences. Gender is understood to be linked to the mind, rather than to one's physical sexual anatomy, and is seen as inherent. As trans activist Janet Mock writes, "'trapped in the wrong body' is a blanket statement that makes trans* people's varying journeys and narratives palatable to the masses." It erases the diversity of trans experience and presents the trans body as disabled, the body a physical deformity. While understanding the lived realities and experiences of these children who dislike their anatomy and desire to change it, I challenge this narrative of disability. In his book *Crip Theory*, Robert McRuer explains how "Compulsory heterosexuality is intertwined with compulsory able-bodiedness; both systems work to (re)produce the able body and heterosexuality" (31). Similarly, these surgeries work to make an able-body where there was a disabled one.

Of course, there is also the fact that while the children are presented as normal within the documentaries, they still require a diagnosis of gender identity disorder in order to receive treatment, and are thus pathologized and labeled with a mental disorder. The forthcoming fifth edition of the *Diagnostic and Statistical Manual of Mental Disorders* (DSM), published by the American Psychiatric Association, will change the diagnosis of "Gender Identity Disorder," which focuses on the mismatch between an individual's identity and behaviour and what is assumed to be their proper gender based on their sexed body, to "Gender Dysporia" which defines the distress and incongruence that many trans people experience around the difference between their gender identity and their sexed bodies. In addition, "Gender Dysphoria" will be removed from the sexual disorders section of the updated DSM. While this change is a step in the right direction because it removes "disorder" from the name and instead focuses on the distress that people feel, it still remains a psychological diagnosis.[6] While keeping some kind of diagnosis in place is preferable some, like Boston Medical Center endocrinologist Dr. Norman Spack, argue that in order to ensure transition care to transgender individuals, gender fluidity should be considered a medical, rather than a psychological issue (Swartz-apfel). It is within these frameworks that parents (and children) manage the medical/psychological narratives as they work to not only explain their children's identities, and also plan for a future in which their children have access to hormones and surgery if they so desire.[7]

BLOGS: ALTERNATIVE STORIES AND DEALING WITH AMBIGUITY

Families show-cased in the media often discuss the need for education as a reason for participating in the documentaries. News stories in the last few years have often quoted the *20/20* special or other shows on transgender children as providing a family with the information they needed to understand their own child. In December 2011, *The Boston Globe* published a story called "Led By the Child Who Simply Knew" that was the catalyst for a ten-year-old in Massachusetts to come out to her mother as Jessie (English). In January 2012, Jessie's mother, Julie Ross, started the blog, *George.Jessie.Love* to chronicle their family's journey.[8] This blog, like the eleven other blogs written by parents of transgender children that I have read, offer narratives around transgender childhood identities and some of the ways in which their families navigate a society that is not always accepting.[9]

Julie Ross recognizes that many people are probably interested in her story for the "juicy" factor. She also acknowledges "Suddenly it became clear to me that while the transgender piece of this is certainly unusual, it actually speaks to everyone's feeling, at some point or another, that they, or perhaps more importantly, their children, are, in their own unique way, just round pegs trying to fit into square holes" ("For Now"). While being fully supportive of Jessie's new identity, Ross shows us the complicated negotiations that occur in relation to school, clothing, friends, as well as the nuances of her own feelings regarding Jessie's identity, particularly around the ambiguity that comes with a child's gender identity. It is hard to not know how the story will end.

This uncertainty is not as clearly defined in the documentaries on transgender children—even though parents are clear about accepting changes, and would allow their children to go back to identifying as their sex assigned at birth if so desired. The way that the narrative is constructed, and the identities presented, makes that possibility seem a slim one.[10] Furthermore, support for these children seems to depend on them not changing their minds. Blogs, such as "George.Jessie.Love," provide a space to demonstrate that having a transgender child is part of a larger narrative: family life, relationships, school, growing up and developing identities and personalities. It is not just about their children's gender identity, transition or medical needs.

The blogosphere also offers a wider range of identities and examples of gender non-conformity, and there are many blogs that address, in more detail, the ways in which parents sometimes have to wait to find out how their children will ultimately identify themselves.[11] Bedford Hope, aka *Accepting Dad*, who writes a blog about his gender non-conforming son, discusses the problem of how media narratives often exclude the experiences of children and parents who find themselves in the middle of the therapeutic spectrum. He writes:

> Confronted with gender non-conforming behaviours, some parents first attempt suppression, suffer with their children through the consequences, and then, they flip; their kid has a birth defect. It's a medical problem. It is gender identity. And it has nothing to do with sexuality. This is the dramatic, unambiguous, civil-rights story that the journalists all tell. In every story—the kid was born

in the wrong body; it's biological. There are boy brains and girl brains; boy bodies and girl bodies. The parents are earnest, unwilling converts, normal people facing this extraordinary challenge.

Hope agrees that "This story is frequently true" but that it doesn't show the whole picture about the complexity of gender fluidity. "Other evidence from across the therapeutic spectrum tells us that some of these kids will identify as trans; some will identify as gay, and some will end up *somewhere in the middle.*" This includes his son, who Hope once assumed was going to be his daughter, and who is now making the choice to go through male puberty. Perhaps his son will be gay, perhaps not; he has not declared a preference yet. Hope discusses the importance of parents listening to their children and holding off any assumptions, and to follow their children's lead. He acknowledges that "ambiguity is hard to deal with" and that it is important to recognize that it is not clear for many families how their child/ren will identify in the next five years or so (Hope 2010).

Along with the difficulty that people have with ambiguity, I propose that this narrative of ambiguity is also viewed as potentially dangerous. If trans children may change their minds, then why let them transition? Why not try to shape their behaviour to be more gender conforming? Dr. Zucker, a Canadian doctor who specializes in gender non-conformity, espouses a therapy that seeks to align children's gendered behaviour with their sex because studies have shown that the majority of boys who are gender non-conforming become gay rather than trans (Rosin). Yet, according to Dr. Olsen ("I Am Jazz") and Dr. Spack (Swartzapfel), this approach is detrimental to those children who need to socially transition in order to survive. Ultimately the narrative of ambiguity is not inherently dangerous to children; it is problematic to a framework where treatment depends on neat definitions of gender identity, gender expression and sexuality.

Anticipation and planning for the future is always part of these narratives, both within the media and within the blogs, yet the idea of possibilities is more evident in some places than in others. *Raising my Rainbow: Adventures in Raising a Fabulously Gender*

Creative Son is a blog that shows ways in which one can support their child without knowing the outcome of their child's gender identity or sexuality, and the importance of opening up possibilities for them and allowing them to figure out their own journey through life. Blogs, such as *Today You are You* and *Life Uncharted* by parents of trans children, also emphasize the importance of listening to children and not foreclosing possibilities.

This is the nature of gender-diverse parenting, which Arywyn Daemyir author of *Raising My Boychick* writes about in her post "10 Myths About Gender Neutral Parenting"; "Today's gender neutral parenting is not about doing away with gender (if it ever really was), but about *doing away with many of the unhealthy pressures around gender*, and *giving our children the freedom to figure out what gender means to them*" (emphasis hers). Here the anticipation inherent within the narrative is not necessarily about avoiding particular outcomes, but rather about opening up options for all children.[12] Similarly, Jane Ward advocates for queer parenting practices that teach "gender self-determination" and "introducing children to the relational and culturally-embedded pleasures associated with gender play, without concretizing a gendered selfhood." She argues that "our project must not center on supporting special children, but on building a movement for all children's gender self-determination" (Chapter 47).

CONCLUSION

This chapter explores the role of anticipation and identity in narratives of transgender and gender-creative children. In my discussion of the narratives within documentaries and blogs, I argue that it is important to keep options open for children and to consider multiple trajectories and possible identities as they grow towards adulthood. While the documentaries challenge assumptions around biology, they continue to affirm particular ideas around gendered norms for boys and girls. Furthermore the psychological and medical explanations around transgender children's gendered expression, sexed bodies, and identities present a singular narrative that ignores the multiplicity of identities, narratives and futures that children may have. In comparison, blogs by parents of transgender and gender creative children contain narratives that are situated within the wider context of family life and offer a more nuanced exploration of children's identities and parents' parenting experiences and choices.

Understanding identity categories as historically contextual, multiple and not-static, is particularly important when considering narratives around children's sexuality and gender. The ways that we understand particular identities such as "gay" or "transgender" and the desirability of each will influence the possible futures that we envision for gender-non-conforming youth. Even as transgender and gay children gain acceptance, particular narratives are still favored over more uncertain/ambiguous ones.

Finally, I argue that one way to address the needs of transgender children is through gender-diverse/queer parenting, especially parenting practices that recognize the fluidity of identity and the myriad future possibilities for children. When Kathy Witterick and David Stocker chose to keep their baby's sex private, they did so envisioning a future of freedom and choice around gender, rather than limitation. I hope that the world that Storm grows up into is one that nourishes children's identities and sense of self, and allows them to express themselves freely.

[1] A type of home schooling that does not follow a set curriculum, but instead follows the child's lead/interests, with the idea that the necessary skills will be learned along the way.

[2] Lesbian, Gay, Bisexual, Transgender, Queer/Questioning

[3] For more discussion of the term transgender, see Valentine; Namaste; Ekins and King; Meyerowitz.

[4] Gender non-conforming and gender variant are terms often found in a psychological, medical and academic setting. Gender-creative is a more positive, or at least value-neutral description, one that Diane Ehrensaft introduces in *Gender Born, Gender Made*, explaining that it is "a developmental position in which the child transcends the culture's normative definitions of male/female to creatively interweave a sense of gender that comes neither totally from the inside (the body, the psyche), nor totally from the outside (the culture, others' perceptions of the child's gender), but resides

somewhere in between." (5). Pink boy and princess boy are terminology I have seen used by parents, such as Cheryl Kilodavis and on *Sarah Hoffman's Blog.*

[5]In general, the TV shows and documentaries tend to focus more on female-identified children than on male identified children. Furthermore, the girls are usually pre-adolescents, whereas most boys are predominantly already teenagers. For more on general demographics of transgender people and an explanation of gender/age dynamics, see Beemyn and Rankin.

[6]For a more detailed analysis and explanation of the changes, see Winters.

[7]For more on parents' narratives about their children's gender identities, see Meadows.

[8]Pseudonym used on the blog.

[9]Blogs by parents of transgender children: *Cammie's Song, George. Jessie.Love, GirlyBoy Mama's Open Salon Blog, "It's Hard to Be Me," My Kennedy's Story, Pasupatidasi's Blog, Today You Are You Blog, Transcendent, Trans*Forming Family, Transforming Love, Transparenthood, Wayne Maine's Huff Post.* These blogs have been gathered over the course of several years of interest and research on gender-creative/queer/trans children, and were found through the Trans Youth Family Allies website, Google searches and Google alerts, as well as through the networks between blogs formed by blogrolls and comment sections. For the most part they are by parents of pre-adolescents, though some of them have children who are currently entering puberty, or are in the beginning of their teenage years.

[10]An exception to this is *In The Life's* "Becoming Me" which focuses on families and their lives with their trans and gender non-conforming children in a way that is not sensationalized or medicalized.

[11]Blogs by parents of gender creative or gay-identified children: *Amelia's Huff Post Gay Voices Blog, Catching Our Rainbow, HE SPARKLES, It's a Bold Life, Labels Are for Jars, Lesbian Dad, Living an Examined Life, My Beautiful Little Boy, Pink Is for Boys, Raising My Rainbow, Raising Queer Kids, Sam's Stories, Sarah Hoffman.* Two of the blogs about transgender children, *It's Hard to Be Me,* and *GirlyBoy Mama,* were originally in this list

of parents with gay and gender creative youth, but their children have since transitioned to a gender identity different than the one they were assigned at birth.

[12]See also Diane Ehrensaft, author of *Gender Born, Gender Made*.

WORKS CITED

"Boys Will Be Girls." ABC *20/20* TV Episode. 2011. Web. Accessed December 17, 2012.

Amelia's Huffington Post Gay Voices Blog. Web. Accessed December 17, 2012.

Adams, Vincanne, Murphy, Michelle, and Adele E. Clarke. "Anticipation: Technoscience, Life, Affect, Temporality." *Subjectivity* 28 (2009): 246-265. Print.

Beemyn, Genny and Susan Rankin. *The Lives of Transgender People*. New York: Columbia University Press, 2011. Print.

Brill, Stephanie A. and Rachel Pepper. *The Transgender Child: A Handbook for Families and Professionals*. San Francisco: Cleis Press, 2008. Print.

Bryant, Karl. "Making Gender Identity Disorder of Childhood: Historical Lessons for Contemporary Debates." *Sexuality Research & Social Policy*. 3.3 (September 2006): 23-39. Print.

Bryant, Karl. "In Defense of Gay Children? 'Progay' Homophobia and the Production of Homonormativity" *Sexualities* 11.4 (August 2008): 455-475. Print.

Cammie's Song. Web. Accessed December 17, 2012.

Catching Our Rainbows. Web. December 17, 2012.

Davis, Lindsay. "Canadian Mother Raising 'Genderless' Baby, Storm, Defends Her Family's Decision" *ABC News*. Web. Accessed December 19, 2011.

Daemyir, Arwyn. "10 Myths About Gender Neutral Parenting" *Raising My Boychick*. 7 June 2011. Web. Accessed December 19, 2011.

D'Emilio, John "Capitalism and Gay Identity." *The Lesbian and Gay Studies Reader*. Eds. Henry Abelove, Michele Aina Barale and David M. Halperin. New York: Routledge, 1993. 467-476. Print.

Dube, Rebecca. "The Mom of a 'Princess Boy' Speaks Out." *TODAY*

Moms. January 3, 2012. Web. Accessed 2 Oct. 2012.

Donaldson James, Susan. "J. Crew Ad With Boy Painting Toenails Pink Stirs Up Transgender Debate." *ABC News* 13 Apr. 2011. Web. Accessed Oct. 29th 2012.

Duggan, Lisa. *The Twilight of Equality? Neoliberalism, Cultural Politics, and the Attack on Democracy.* Boston: Beacon Press, 2004. Print.

Ehrensaft, Diane. *Gender Born, Gender Made: Raising Healthy Gender Non-conforming Children.* New York: The Experiment, 2011. Print.

Ekins, Richard and Dave King. *The Phenomenon of Transgender.* Thousand Oaks: Sage, 2006. Print.

English, Bella. "Led By the Child Who Simply Knew" *The Boston Globe*. December 2011. Web.

Dangling Possibilities. Web. Accessed December 17, 2012.

Dvorak, Petula. "Transgender at Five." *The Washington Post* 21 May 2012. Web. Accessed 2 Oct. 2012.

Fitzpatrick, Laura. "The Gender Conundrum." *Time* 8 Nov. 2007. Web. Accessed 25 Apr. 2012.

Foucault, Michel. *The History of Sexuality: An Introduction, Vol. 1.* New York: Random House, 1978. Print.

GirlyBoy Mama's Open Salon Blog. Web. Accessed December 17, 2012.

Green, Jesse. "S/He" *New York Magazine*. May 27, 2012. Web. Accessed December 17, 2012.

Gorman, Anna. "Transgender Kids Get Help Navigating a Difficult Path." *Los Angeles Times* 15 June 2012. Print.

Harris, Sean. "Official Statement of Retraction." May 2, 2012. Web. Accessed December 17, 2012.

HE SPARKLES. Web. Accessed December 17, 2012.

Hooper, Jason. "Video: Amendment 1 Pastor Gives Parents "special dispensation" to use violence against LGBT Kids" May 1, 2012. Web. Accessed October 2· 2012.

Hope, Bedford. "Trans kids, the Media, and the Excluded Middle." *Accepting Dad*. September 22, 2009. Web. Accessed December 19, 2011.

Hope, Bedford. "When the Girliest of Girls Turn Out To Be Men." 4 March 2010. Web. Accessed December 19, 2011.

"I am Jazz: A Family in Transition." Dir. Jennifer Stocks. *OWN*. Aired 27 November 2011. Figure 8 Films.

It's A Bold Life. Web. Accessed December 17, 2012.

It's Hard to Be Me: Parenting and Loving Our Gender Fluid Child. Web. Accessed December 17, 2012.

Labels Are for Jars. Web. Accessed December 17, 2012.

Lesbian Dad. Web. Accessed December 17, 2012.

Life Uncharted. Web. Accessed December 19, 2011.

Ling, Lisa. "Transgender Lives." *Our America*. The Oprah Winfrey Network. February 22, 2011.

Living An Examined Life. Web. Accessed December 17, 2012.

Kilodavis, Cheryl. *My Princess Boy*. Illustrated by Suzanne DeSimone. New York: Aladdin, 2010. Print.

Manual, Emily. "Guest Post: Why Does the Media Show Transgender Children more Sympathetically?" *Raising My Boychick*. October 2 2011. Web. Accessed December 19, 2011.

Meadows, Tey. "Deep Down Where the Music Plays: How Parents Account for Childhood Gender Variance" *Sexualities* 14.6 (2011): 725-747. 2011. Print.

Meyerowitz, Joanne. *How Sex Changed: A History of Transsexuality in the United States*. Cambridge: Harvard University Press, 2002. Print.

McRuer, Robert. *Crip Theory: Cultural Signs of Queerness and Disability*. New York: New York University Press, 2006. Print.

Mock, Janet. "Trans Media: Unlearning the "Trapped" Metaphor and Taking Control of Our Bodies" *Fish Food for Thought* July 9, 2012. Web. Accessed October 31, 2012.

Murdoch, Cassie. "Horrible Pastor Advocates Beating The Gay Out of Young Kids" *Jezebel Blog* May 2, 2012. Web. Accessed October 15, 2012.

My Beautiful Little Boy. Web. Accessed December 17, 2012.

My Kennedy's Story. Web. Accessed December 17, 2012.

"My Secret Self: A Story of Transgender Children." ABC *20/20* TV Episode. Aired 27 April 2007.

Namaste, Vivian K. *Invisible Lives: The Erasure of Transsexual and Transgendered People*. Chicago: Chicago University Press, 2000. Print.

Padawer, Ruth. "What's So Bad About a Boy Who Wants to Wear

a Dress?" *New York Times*. August 8, 2012. Web. Accessed 2 Oct. 2012.

Pasupatidasi's Blog. Web. Accessed December 17, 2012.

Park, Madison. "Transgender Children: Painful Quest to Be Who They Are." CNN.Com. September 27th 2011. Web. Accessed December 19, 2011.

Pickert, Nils. "Lebenslagen. Kinder & Jugendliche. Vater Im Rock." *Emma* 20 Aug. 2012. Web. Accessed 29 Oct. 2012.

Pink is for Boys. Web. Accessed December 17, 2012.

Poisson, Jayme. "Parents Keep Child's Gender Secret." *Toronto Star.* May 21, 2011a. Web. Accessed December 19, 2011.

Poisson, Jayme. "*Star* Readers Rage About Couple Raising 'Genderless' Infant." *Toronto Star* May 24, 2011b. Web. Accessed December 19, 2011.

Raising My Rainbow. Web. Accessed December 17, 2012.

Raising Queer Kids. Web. Accessed December 17, 2012.

Rosin, Hanna. "A Boy's Life." *The Atlantic.* Nov. 2008. Web. Accessed December 17, 2012.

Ross, Julie. *George. Jessie. Love. Parenting and Loving a Transgender Kid.* Web. Accessed December 17, 2012.

Ross, Julie. "For Now." *George. Jessie. Love. Parenting and Loving a Transgender Kid.* Web. Accessed December 17, 2012.

Sam's Stories. Web. Accessed December 17, 2012.

Sarah Hoffman: On Parenting A Boy Who is Different. Web. Accessed December 17, 2012.

Stockton, Kathryn Bond. *The Queer Child, or Growing Sideways in the Twentieth Century*. Durham: Duke University Press Books, 2009. Print.

Swartzapfel, Beth. "How Norman Spack Transformed the Way We Treat Transgender Children." *The Phoenix*. August 10, 2012. Web. Accessed December 17, 2012.

"Too Young to Know Your Gender?" CNN 27 September 2011. Web. Accessed December 19, 2011.

Transcendent: Reflections on Raising A Transgender Child. Web. Accessed December 17, 2012.

*Trans*Forming Family*. Web. Accessed December 17, 2012.

Transforming Love: Support for Mothers of Transgender Children. Web. Accessed December 17, 2012.

Transparenthood: Experiences Raising a Transgender Child. Web. Accessed December 17, 2012.

Trans Youth Family Allies Website. Web. Accessed December 17, 2012.

Today You Are You. Web. Accessed December 19, 2011.

Valentine, David. *Imagining Transgender: An Ethnography of a Category*. Durham: Duke University Press, 2007. Print.

Ward, Jane. "Get Your Gender Binary Off My Childhood! Towards a Movement for Children's Self-Determination." *Chasing Rainbows: Exploring Gender Fluid Parenting Practices*. Eds. Fiona Joy Green and May Friedman. Bradford, ON: Demeter Press, 2013. 43-52. Print.

Wayne Maine's Huffington Post Blog. Web. Accessed December 17, 2012.

Warner, Michael. *The Trouble With Normal: Sex, Politics, and the Ethics of Queer Life*. New York: Free Press, 1999. Print.

Winters, Kelley. "An Update on Gender Diagnoses as the DSM 5 Goes to Press" *GID Reform Weblog by Kelley Winters*. Web. Accessed December 17, 2012.

6.
We're Having a Stanley

J WALLACE

THE SUMMER I WAS THIRTEEN, my eldest cousin got married. She asked all the female cousins to be bridesmaids, and they all wore Little-Bo-Peep dresses modelled on the dresses Lady Diana's bridesmaids wore for her fairytale wedding. All the female cousins, except me. Ostensibly it was because my hair didn't match the colour scheme—all the others had blond hair, and I had mouse brown hair, but I think the hair excuse was invented because no one wanted to tell me the truth—she didn't want to have a drag queen as a bridesmaid. It was perhaps the first time my gender was recognized at a family event, and while nobody said I was a boy, it was clear no one recognized me as a girl either.

I was lucky to be born in the seventies, and raised on *Free to Be ... You and Me.* When I was very small, nobody questioned that a girl-child might only ever ask for Lego and a pocket-knife for presents. My middle school did not have a girls' soccer team, and when I was unable to get the phys. ed. teacher to launch one, I argued that I should at least be allowed to try out for the boys' team. At home, this was interpreted as "being a good feminist," and not a failure of femininity. While I had no idea that transpeople existed, or that one could choose to be a man or a woman, or both, or neither, throughout my childhood I was encouraged to choose what kind of a girl I wanted to be, and not to see anything as off limits. If I was cataloguing the things I appreciate about how my parents raised me, this freedom to choose would top the list.

Before my husband and I became parents, we spent a great deal of time talking about the kind of parents we wanted to be. We spent hours upon hours negotiating about all manner of parenting values, but I don't remember us talking about gender. For us, it was so clear that we wanted to raise a small person with gender choices that we did not even need to talk about it—the same way, as two Anglophones, we did not negotiate about raising our child in English. Now, because other people ask (and keep asking), I can articulate some of the pieces: I want our small person to have choices, I am interested in encouraging self expression and self exploration, I will make sure there is space for possibility, and I want our small person to feel celebrated. We parent with these values because it is how we live in the world, and the work we both do. We parent with these values, not because we are making some particular "gender experiment" out of our child, but because all parenting is a "gender experiment" and having been tested by several possibilities ourselves we believe this is best.

We called our journey towards parenthood "The Small Person Acquisition Project,"[1] and our first concrete step was to choose a name. Some parents talk about how they negotiated over a name, or how they had several they liked, we were always clear that we were having a Stanley. Stanley is a family name from both sides of the family—both my husband and I had grandfathers named Stanley to whom we were particularly close, and before you ask, no, not the same grandfather, although they died within six weeks of each other during the year we met. We were having a Stanley. Other people were immediately concerned—"What if you have a girl?" they demanded, to which we would blithely respond, "We'll call her Stanley." Mentioning that Barak Obama's mother's name is Stanley usually settled people down. Nobody asked "What if you have a boy?

Throughout the period between conception and birth, when asked if we knew what we were having, we would respond with great gladness "A baby!" It's true, we had seen the baby's genitals on an ultrasound, but that felt like private information for just the two of us. I had not anticipated how persistent people would be in asking this question, how frustrating people found it when we would not say if we were having a "boy or a girl." Some people asked if we were joining "team pink or team blue" and seemed offended when we responded that we were joining "team baby." It meant that people scrutinized our plans, our baby registry and our baby-related purchases to see if they could find clues about the baby's sex. When people understood clearly that we were not going to tell them if we were expecting a girl or a boy, they would offer to buy us yellow things, and we would have to gently explain that we were not looking to expand the binary of boy = blue and girl = pink to three options, but that we wanted our child to have access to the full colour wheel, and that with time, our child could choose what colours to wear.

My friend Max talks about how while he was pregnant, he was read more and more often as female—and that he dealt with this by preserving a space outside of people's gender expectations for his coming baby. To me, baby is a word without a gender, almost as if "baby" is its own gender. "Baby" has possibilities, and I want to preserve those possibilities for as long as I can. Retailers, however, are interested in asserting gender categories as soon as possible. I was amazed to discover that stores were literally divided into pink and blue sections, often with the floor tiles and walls colour-coded to prevent even a sleep deprived parent from ending up in the wrong part of the store.

We've had a few rules about clothing from the very beginning, and none is about outlawing pink and blue. Rule one has been nothing that sexualizes children, both because the very notion disturbs us, but also because so often this clearly is intended to reinforce heterosexuality. So, no "Daddy's Little Sweetheart" with big red lipstick prints, no shirts from the boy's section reading "Get In Line Girls," no "Daddy's Little Flirt." Rule two has been no messages that reinforce stereotypical gender roles. So, while the boy's section offers "Mommy's Hero" and "Daddy's Little Helper" we leave both of them on the rack. We've avoided clothing from the boys' section that glorifies sports and trucks, and we've avoided clothing from the girls' that's all bows and ruffles and bearing messages about being nothing but pretty. We've valued comfort, playfulness, and things that we think are appealing (which has resulted in a greater-than-average number of both octopi and bicycles represented in Stanley's wardrobe).

We've accepted a great many hand-me-downs, and shopped on both sides of stores.

It's important to me to note here that this is not about ignoring gender or trying to get rid of the categories of "boy" and "girl" and replace them with a single one labelled "gender neutral." Because neither of us are femme, we've had long conversations about whom, if our child turns out to be femme in gender, might be able to provide guidance in the femme-ly arts and sciences. My husband is a bit of a dandy, with an interest in pocket squares, cuff links and bow ties; I'm a bit urban-queer-meets-farmer. While both of us appreciate femme, neither one of us have ever been particularly skilled at embodying it. A cadre of strong femmes of our acquaintance and affection stepped forward to offer assistance. At the moment, Stanley has bright pink shirts, a tutu, all manner of leggings, a pink straw hat, and a very sparkly collection of hair clips to sport in those blond ringlets. If femme turns out to be what Stanley wants we'll expand upon this. I'm aware that parents who are trying to avoid gender stereotypes in children's clothing often end up shopping from the boy's side of the store and that while pants can be seen as "gender neutral" skirts never get that designation. I'm cautious that our choices are about choosing things we like, and preserving choice for Stanley, and not merely in doing away with the extremes. I am not sure we understood, when we undertook the process of child-making, how much resistance it would require to keep a space of choice for Stanley, but the pressure is there, and the harder marketing departments try to enforce gender the more vigour we give to the resistance.

The grown people around here are by-and-large a pants wearing bunch. We got married in kilts, and do wear kilts for fancy occasions. We've been known to sport sarongs, but generally folded as men fold them. If we were Stanley's only role models this might be a problem, but we're not. Stanley knows people who wear dresses and skirts and look fabulous in them. A whole legion of people he looks up to and respects, including family members, day-care providers and friends model that these are fine clothing choices. If we as parents are modelling choice about what feels comfortable and appropriate for us, we're not going to start wearing skirts to model that they are particularly fine choices, but we are going to model choosing. For what it's worth, I also avoid neckties, dislike vests and prefer gloves over mittens. It's possible Stanley is a little light on role models who wear ties, but other than that we are doing just fine.

At two-and-a-half Stanley is just beginning to express desires in clothes. Most of the time, Stanley is content to make choices from the clothes we've provided, but Stanley has just begun making requests for new clothing. We have been informed that there are not enough purple shirts, and in the spirit of honouring choice we're getting more purple shirts. Stanley has a clear preference for soft pants and tends to balk at jeans, so we choose pants and shorts in soft cotton jersey, regardless of what gender of child the designer might have imagined. In general, Stanley goes out in the world with animals on his chest, sturdy shoes on his feet, long gorgeous hair and perfect confidence in his choices.

Perhaps you found that last sentence a relief—perhaps you are glad that I've finally acknowledged Stanley's gender. Perhaps you've been waiting for that and wondering. At my most recent check, Stanley told me that he's "a boy," although she's also said she's "a girl," and ze's declared that ze is a "toddler" and "a big kid." My favourite Stanley gender statement came one evening, after reading Jacinta Bunnell's *Girls Will Be Boys Will Be Girls* when Stanley declared, "My gender is purple." Stanley's declared gender changes day to day, and I try not to put too much stock in today's answer. The same way I try not to put too much stock in him loving macaroni cheese and fresh peas today; toddlers are known for being mercurial, and tomorrow always could be different. In both cases, with gender and dinner, it is immensely important that I value his understanding of himself in the moment, and equally important that I not project this far into his future. He gets to tell me what is right for him right now, and I get to understand that at a different, future, now this might change. Even with all these declarations, I'm not sure he understands gender yet—he applies "he" and "she" to people without discernible pattern. We're teaching him that you know what pronoun to use by asking the person you want to talk about.

Children's clothing stores are not the only gender-segregated places we find ourselves in. Try selecting a book or a toy for a child, and the person assisting you is most likely to ask you "Is this for a girl or a boy?" It takes a daily effort to describe Stanley as "a curious small person, full of wonder in the world and enthusiasm," rather than a girl or a boy, but it feels so important not to limit his potential—or his playthings—because of his gender.

Our thoughts about gender were present in our search for a day-care. First, we needed one where he would be able to celebrate his two-dad family, where they would respect and encourage children of all genders to learn to be caring nurturers, and not pity him for not having a mother. Second we needed one that would let him play without gendered restrictions. The day we toured the day-care we would eventually choose, there were two children fighting over a purse. When the staff person intervened, she said "Derek, Simon has the purse right now, he's having his turn, you can have it when he's finished." There was no shaming of either boy for wanting a purse, no suggestion that it was inappropriate. Just a call to share.

At his day care they call him "The Blond Earthquake," acknowledging both what a force of nature he is and his long blond hair. We've never cut Stanley's hair, and his beautiful ringlets fall halfway to his waist. When we are out in public, most people seem to see his hair as his defining gender signifier, and compliment us on "what a beautiful girl" we have. It's a challenge to disrupt their assumption that long hair means girl, and that all girls should be pretty, without teaching Stanley that it would be wrong to be a girl, or without being rude in the face of a compliment. I also don't think that Stanley understands why people think he's a girl because he has long hair. I don't think he knows enough long-haired women or short-haired men to understand many people assume a correlation. Some days, at day-care, they play Hair Studio. The staff get out elastics and clips, and style the children's hair. It's a quiet activity, where a child can snuggle up with a staff person and come away feeling tended to and beautiful, which seems like a good thing for any child. Stanley loves Hair Studio days.

Our thoughts on gender have also impacted our media choices—mostly that we don't. We don't have a television, and we don't engage with the Disney Empire. He is slowly discovering Dora the Explorer and Thomas the Tank Engine through other children, but his imagination is not populated by such things yet. We populate his imagination with a great diversity of characters from a great many books. In time there will be more television, I am sure, and commercial toy crazes—and he'll catch up. I don't imagine that we can keep him from these things forever. I do imagine, in my best and most hopeful heart, that for now, he gets to create all the action and all the storylines. I imagine that this is how you make storytellers; you feed them lots of pieces of books and let them play with the ideas.

As a grown person, I find I can do all the thinking I want on a particular topic, and then I go out in the world, and what I have thought about ahead of time becomes less important that what I do in the moment. On a recent weekend, Stanley and I were camping at a music festival. The tents were pitched close together, there was accordion and fiddle music, and a gaggle of kids played together between the tents. One of them, who looked to be about five-years-old, stopped and asked me if Stanley was a boy or a girl. I looked at Stanley, and called out "Stanley, are you a girl or a boy?" Stanley responded "I'm a girl." So I repeated this to the girl who asked and the two of them went back to the very serious kid business of running around, chasing beach balls, yelling and trying to get adults to pull them around in carts.

It was about perhaps fifteen minutes later that I heard the child introducing Stanley to her mother. "This is Stanley," said the child, "she's a girl."

The parent gently responded, "Stanley's a boy's name honey, I don't think you've got that right."

Stanley, who was sitting in the cart with the child and next to the mother, chimed in: "I'm a girl!"

The mother however, rather than take her child's word on it, or my child's corroboration, engaged in a bit of a back-and-forth with the kids, insisting that Stanley must be a boy. Eventually she looked over to where I was washing dishes and asked: "Is Stanley a boy or a girl?"

I responded, "She says she's a girl, so she's a girl!"

The mother however, was not quite willing to take my word on it either. "But isn't Stanley a boy's name?" she asked.

So I told her the story of how we had picked the name Stanley before Stanley was conceived, and that we decided we were having a Stanley, regardless of sex. I shared our go-to tidbit that Barack Obama's mother's first name is Stanley, and we left it at that.

I've been thinking about the series of exchanges since. First, parenting is a constant series of small moments and decisions. I'm glad that when the small child asked me if Stanley was a boy or a girl my impulse was to ask Stanley. I like that it reinforces both that there is a choice, and that Stanley is the one who gets to make that choice. I like that it makes Stanley and not me the expert on Stanley. I like that it lets Stanley choose in that moment what identity feels best. I don't always feel so good about my parenting, but in this moment, I found the right answer, and I want to hold on to it, and remember it so I can use it again.

Later that morning, another child came to hang out with me as I packed up our stuff. This other child was interested in our things, and kept asking what things were. At first I was annoyed, as I wanted to get the dry gear packed before it rained and was trying to keep track of my child. I thought the child was just hanging out with me for something to do—then the child said, "Don't mistake me for a girl. Lots of people mistake me for a girl." Suddenly, it was clear to me why this child was hanging out with me. "I won't," I said. The child told me that because he has long hair, and painted nails, many people think he's a girl. "Wait until you see my costume for the parade" he said, and because the children's parade was soon, he went away and got dressed. When he returned he was in a lacy white dress—the kind of dress I imagine a child might wear for first communion—and was sporting a giant pair of boxing gloves. "You look fabulous and fierce," I said, and he seemed delighted. Both in the moment, and as I write this, I recognise that I am both like the child, and the mother across the way. Like the child, I want to define my own gender, and find the one that fits best is often a little queer. Like the mother, I was tempted both then, and now writing about it, to make guesses about what sex the child was assigned at birth.

I recognize this as my adultism, my own inappropriate curiosity, and how steeped I am in our culture's understanding of gender. It would not have been appropriate to ask him, or to guess that morning, the only right answer was to do as he asked, and "not mistake him for a girl," and it would be even less appropriate to make guesses now in his absence. Let me just say that he was fierce, and fabulous, and that he asked me to get it right. I want to do that, for him. I want to make sure he is able to keep finding places he can demand that adults get his gender right, and I want to make sure that we do. Ultimately this is what I want for all of us, children and grown people, that we are able to assert who we are, and that the people who are near us listen, believe and act accordingly. I hope that the choices we are making in raising Stanley will make this easier for Stanley than it ever has been for me.

[1]We also used this title for a CBC radio documentary about our journey toward parenthood. The documentary can be heard at: <http://www.cbc.ca/thecurrent/episode/2010/12/24/small-person-acquisition>.

WORKS CITED

Bunnell, Jacinta and Irit Reinheimer. *Girls Will Be Boys Will Be Girls Will Be ... A Colouring Book*. Brooklyn: Soft Skull Press. 2004. Print.

Thomas, Marlo. *Free To Be ... You And Me*. Philadelphia: Running Press Publishers. 1974. Print.

7.
Between the Village
and The Village People

Negotiating Community, Ethnicity and Safety
in Gender Fluid Parenting

MAY FRIEDMAN

"WHY DON'T YOU JUST BUY HIM A GUN? It would be just as dangerous!" This is my mother's impassioned response to my decision to allow my four-year-old son to wear a skirt.

Although I am explicit about my feminist values and have attempted to raise my children in a gender fluid context, this is the moment where all of the vague allusions I have made come to a head, where all the dolls and trucks for my sons and daughter unambiguously solidify into a message my mother finally can't ignore: I am going to honour my small son's sartorial decision-making and allow him to wear "girls'" clothing. All the groundwork I had thought I'd laid over the years has obviously not made the impression I expected because my mother is exactly as shocked as she would have been had I given my boy a loaded gun.

I attempt to weakly deflect her anger, to shield my children from her outrage, to explain my commitment to this value system, but leave her house with a sick feeling in the pit of my stomach. My mother, notorious for calling me multiple times a day, does not communicate with me for more than a week and takes weeks longer to drop her frosty tone.

There are a number of ways to read this interaction. On the one hand, it is easy to give a simple reading: my mother, an older, immigrant woman, is unfamiliar with contemporary outlooks on gender and is thus amusingly outraged by this most gentle of forays into gender fluidity. A more nuanced response would look at the oppression and danger she experienced in her countries of origin and would respond to her passion as a natural extension of her complicated life history. Alternately, we may examine my mother's strongly normative gender identity as a safety blanket as her other identities (age, citizenship, ethnicity) have been shifting and unstable.

All of these readings of our conversation are true, and yet none are adequate, none address how bereft I feel at her scorn and fury, or how complicated are the intricacies of our relationship, and of her relationship to her grandson and subsequent grandchildren. These readings are also not the story I want to tell, of the simple uneducated Orientalized immigrant woman who doesn't "get" "our" enlightened values (Arat-Koç). That reading is both disrespectful to my mother (and my roots) and doesn't acknowledge the force of our familial ties.

If there is a village raising my children, my mother is on the town council. She is a central part of our lives, and the tension between the need for her support and her inability—for whatever reason—to share my parenting values cannot be read as her "simpleness." The truth is far from simple.

SHARING THE CARING

How do we take care? How can we ensure that our children live safe and authentic lives? I increasingly find myself with two competing and contradictory responses to this question. Answer one says that we cannot provide safety alone, that mythic nuclear families are simply insufficient to provide for the complex needs of children, and indeed, their parents (Kinser). The second answer, however, is the answer that comes when I am frightened. When I am made aware of my race, I want to protect my children from racism. When I fear the repercussions of living in a female body, I want to surround them with enlightened feminists. And when they explore their gender diversity, using the tools I have been trying to give them for years, I am shocked by my own hesitation, my own fear and desire to limit their environment to safe allies. Yet to do so is to court disaster in other realms.

I've written about our need to assume responsibility for one another, as individuals, families, and communities (Friedman). As a social work academic, I am strongly committed to the notion of shared responsibility culminating in the formal response of a robust welfare state. I believe that we all experience contingencies in our lives and that having a strong societal support system (not merely the informal networks of family and friends) is essential to our continued well-being (Baines). This is especially so in the wearying realm of parenthood where liberal individualism would have us, mothers in particular, assume sole responsibility for the avalanche of minutiae associated with maintaining life and socializing small humans (O'Reilly). On a political level, I advocate for national childcare, state support for single mothers and other impoverished parents. On both instrumental and psychological levels, I do not believe we were meant to go it alone. This can be seen in my parenting practice, in my attempt to ensure that my children experience multiple secure attachments to their caregivers. Aiming to disrupt the perceived normativity of our immediate family, we discuss our kids' "grown-ups"—Mama, Daddy, Safta, Saba, Sabrina, Doda Judy, Bubie, Zadie, their teachers, our neighbours, friends, etc. And indeed, especially in their infancies, it felt like we were able to participate in a nuanced patchwork of caregiving, assisted by those around us in negotiating the work of sustaining young life.

It may seem that my commitment to this shared and communal parenting practice is born from ideology, yet, like all praxis, it begins with very tangible realities: in my case, the reality of blending complicated and intense employment with a desire for multiple children. I can no longer say whether my commitment to communality grew with my family or allowed my family to grow, yet here we are with many, many allies in our parenting (though of course, the final burdens of total responsibility, and the legal assignment of liability remain my partner's and mine alone). What I could not foresee as my children's needs grew beyond immediate physical care and increasingly into the realm of political and emotional choices, was the impact of diversifying their care team beyond our intimate bubble. If we share their care, we have a different responsibility to allow others to weigh in on parenting choices, a notion that is anathema in a neo-liberal environment that controls parental choice through dominant discourse, but purports to leave the transmission of values to parents alone. When my children were tiny, I would have blithely agreed that monolithic parental control was both unrealistic and not in children's best interest. Then I bought my son a skirt.

FEMINISM AS A SECOND LANGUAGE

I did not grow up with feminism. Unlike many of my friends and colleagues who became politicized in childhood or adolescence, who attended protests and discussed the intersections of personal and political with their families of origin, my consciousness was raised at a much later stage. It was not until graduate school (shortly after my enormous spectacle of a wedding, complete with name change) that my "click" moment occurred. Suddenly, I found language to describe the nagging discomfort I had felt for years, the vague recognition that things were not as they should be. My indistinct commitment to a moral life was abruptly reconfigured as a strong dedication to social justice.

The contemporary feminism that I espouse engages with critical race theory and a reckoning of both heterosexism and homophobia, considers the social model of disability and (less than I'd like) the impact of class (Hernandez and Rehman; Wilson, Sengupta and Evans); it functions as "a polysemic site of contradictory position-alities" (Shohat 2). This post-structuralist, post-colonial moment has allowed me to make sense of my own life and identity as well as the complex world I inhabit. My engagement with feminism thus affected my parenting before I even began to grow my family. I knew the impact of gender, race and class on my own life; I could see more clearly my areas of privilege. Most of all, I wanted to live an empowered life despite motherhood, and wanted to ensure that my children had complete access to all opportunities and experiences, regardless of their sex or gender. My commitment to these ideals grew quickly alongside my parenting. I was frustrated at the extent to which becoming parents allowed my relationship with my partner to regress to problematic gender roles (though years of provocative conversation have had a remarkable impact on these concerns). I was, and am, incredibly dismayed at the limitations placed on my older son and daughter in particular, the extent to which my son has been dubbed smart and strong, lauded for his physical ability, while my daughter is praised for her beautiful penmanship (pengirlship?) and capacity for independent play. One of the many joys of welcoming our third child was the extent to which this little person was allowed a distinct personality without every trait, every difference from his siblings, being immediately put down to sex.

Co-parenting with my partner has itself required intense negotiation, and an awareness of the ways that parenting in a heterosexual union presents its own version of gender entrenchment. His martial arts training, my baking, my preference for laundry while he takes out the garbage—these hobbies and chores are not benign choices. Likewise, when we play to our strengths as parents, my children may view their female parent doing detail oriented work and keeping track of things like appointments and deadlines, while their male parent may sometimes seem like more fun. On the other hand, there are ways we subvert these binaries, make choices that work against expectations. Certainly, we stand together in our attempts to maintain an awareness of the ways that gender works on us and with us as parents, and as people.

Gender fluid parenting isn't about letting them wear each the "other" gender's clothes, though of course, we encourage them to do so. It isn't about buying them dolls and trucks. It's about aiming for ongoing complicated conversations that encourage them to understand how their ideas and identities are formed. It's about helping them keep doors open, to allow them to become their most authentic selves. This involves an exploration of race, of ability, a consideration of the reading of my fat, brown body and their white skin and the ways other identities intersect with gender. It's about asserting both the centrality of gender on their lives, and, simultaneously, its fundamental irrelevance.

These are radical values, ideas that are fundamentally contrary to the dominant discourses about how boys and girls, and mothers and fathers, *should* act. It's an uphill battle to uphold these values in the face of school, media, peers and virtually all other influences blaring the need for specific and delineated gender that matches genitalia, to encourage critical thought instead of mindless conformity. As Dan Kois asserts, "…any parent raising kids in 2012 knows that it's still not simple navigating a culture that seems intent on selling princess dresses to girls (even if the princesses who wear them are spunky, smart, and Brave) and superhero outfits to boys (even if the superheroes are—well, they're pretty much still all muscly dudes)." It is tempting to believe that I am best served by protecting my kids as much as possible from the influence of the outside world, by aiming to limit their loving relationships to only myself and my co-parent, or perhaps a tiny circle of allies. Yet to do so works in direct conflict with my aim to remained empowered as a mother. In my particular context, empowered motherhood is achieved by allowing my children to be bombarded with love, by inviting the people in my family and community to join me in caring for these young people. Asking for help, asking for community, however, makes the "values" message less coherent, and, especially in the case of intimate caregivers like my mother, requires that I cede control, that I grant buy-in. I cannot share my children solely on my terms without severely restricting my access to both instrumental and emotional support.

HAVING IT ALL

Suggesting that my children benefit from a wealth of caregivers only to give me a break diminishes the full potential of these contradictory and complicated relationships. By spending time with many people who love them, my children have learned to embrace ambiguity, to understand (respectful) conflict, and have had their certainty about adult omnipotence severely challenged. Arguably, their capacity for critical thought has been extended by their access to so many different points of view. They have learned about things that I cannot teach them. When they talk to their grandfather about how he left his whole family behind to avoid remaining a soldier, they learn about gender. When they learn about their grandmother's experiences in law school while parenting their father as a young child, they learn about heteronormativity. When they witness, or talk to their aunt about her decision to parent her children in a hyper-gendered way, they are exercising their critical capacity to understand how gender marks our beliefs and intersects with systems such as religion and class. Both positive and negative influences thus allow my children to learn much more than they would if I restricted them, by some wizardry, to a perfect progressive enclave. Yet such an analysis does not take into account their safety, the ways that I flinch when a family member says something homophobic, or how I recoil when the conversation turns to a patronizing analysis of racialized nannies, and the trouble with finding "good help." I am looking for "good help," and I am frightened of the implications of sharing my children with people who love them, but who do not express that love in terms of acceptance or respect for difference. I am especially fearful of the implications of normative gender models, given the high rate of suicide among gender diverse young people: Kim Pearson, of the Trans Youth Family Allies suggests that, "Trans kids are the highest suicide risk on the planet, bar none" (quoted in Green). I cannot say whether my children will push beyond the limits of the sexes listed on their birth certificates, but I will be damned if I will lose them because they are afraid to.

Given the impossibility of "safe space," I nonetheless want to help my children avoid hateful influences, to feel free to explore their potential, especially with people who purport to love them. It is sometimes tempting to limit access in the name of safety. As I navigate this terrain, I realize the extent to which I remain closeted about my beliefs and desires in the heart of my family of origin. I take note of the ways that my decision to partner with a man has allowed me to "pass" for so long that I have forgotten the depth of the normativity with which I was raised. Yet to portray my origins as normative is also a distortion, also doesn't tell the whole story.

OUTSIDE/IN

Some days it feels like I live my life in two modes. I am the confident feminist academic, examining representations of motherhood in the public sphere and teaching my students about the perils of hegemonic identity markers. Other times, however, I'm just "Baby May."

"Baby May" is the way I'm known in my family of origin. Nine years younger than my only sibling, I will never not be the baby, no matter how many degrees I get or children I bear. And because sometimes I am weary of arguing, it is sometimes comforting to retreat to this place, a place where critical thought is given much less value than high fashion.

Coming from extreme poverty, racism and marginalization, the class privilege that my family of origin has achieved is tempered by insecurity, by experiences as both refugees and immigrants. Our shifting geographical base has prioritized our familial connections, which may be why being "Baby May" is so seductive, so safe. In their own ways, my family and community of origin is quite politicized but are often very conservative as a means of erasing their past vulnerabilities and maintaining their own need for untouchable safety in the present day. Their biases and hostilities toward my progressive beliefs are not borne of ignorance, but of a complex amalgam of fear, history and love—of a feeling that their conservatism will save my children and me the pain of being an outsider, of being reviled for my identity. Bizarrely, in my particular experience, my family and I are attempting to solve the same problem—responding to difference—by enacting two opposing solutions. I attempt to embrace difference and fluidity in gender, sexuality, and in all other realms. They smile grimly at my naiveté and advise me, in their words and their actions, to avoid standing out, to annihilate difference whenever possible and to "pass" for as long as I can.

The conservatism of my places of origin makes me deeply uncomfortable, but it is its own sort of home. By contrast, emigrating to my progressive neighbourhood downtown has surrounded me with parenting allies, with hip gender-bending kids on the monkey bars at our local park. Yet this shift has not always been perfectly comfortable. In some respects I feel unstably situated in this domain, surrounded by relatively class-privileged and educated (and overwhelming white) neighbours. As Paula Austin beautifully articulates, "I have felt left out of feminism mostly because it leaves out women who looked like my mother" (167). Like others who inhabit liminal identities (Walker; Weiner-Mahfuz), sometimes I feel like an outlier wherever I dwell.

I fear that by analyzing my own experiences, I lend fuel to the stereotypical construction of raised consciousness as solely the domain of privileged bodies, and of gender fluidity as exclusively a white enterprise (Tokawa). I cringe a bit when I am admired for my parenting practice, when I hear "they are so lucky to have you!" The cringing is because I am merely muddling my way through, making endless, future-therapy-inducing errors, scolding when I should listen, pushing away when I should gather my children close, wrestling with the challenge of being myself and being account-able. I can't hear that I'm doing this well when I know how many ways I may be parenting poorly. At the same time, however, there is a deeper discomfort behind my resistance to acknowledging the praise of my parenting practice: especially when issued in response to my concerns about difficult moments with other loved ones and caregivers, these accolades feel fraught. Sometimes it feels like the subtext of the compliment is an acknowledgement that we are so much more enlightened than our forebears; that we are more educated than the people around us.

As someone who did not grow up steeped in feminism, this anal-ysis makes me squirm. It feels like so recently that I was the person making ham-handed comments, that I could so easily have stayed in my well-intentioned, charity model, uncritical compassion. I am aware of the ways that the rhetoric, in my case, may be true—that I have had my consciousness raised through education, and that that is an unearned and complicated privilege. I am also aware of the politicization of many of the people around me through sites of extreme oppression, of my immigrant and Aboriginal colleagues who understand "revolution" in visceral ways that I will never access, of my marginalized friends who know the meaning of activism in their bodies, in tangible and critical moments. I don't want to write the story of the educated English speaking daugh-ter who raises her kids "right," protecting them from the biased and unenlightened views of her immigrant parents. That story is limited and limiting and does everyone, my parents, my children and myself, a great disservice.

My resistance to the notion of gender fluid parenting as exclusively the domain of educated Western parents does not merely take issue with this supposition as a misrepresentation of the many forms of complicated gender expression that occur in non-Western contexts (Comeau). Rather, on a personal level, I fear my children becoming entitled to activism. Suddenly, I am raising the people who will blithely discuss the protests they attended with their mama, who will take for granted the need for social transformation. In this context, it can be easy to raise children who will becoming unthinkingly critical, who will develop a critical lens that may not be informed by the hard work of consciousness raising, but will instead merely allow them to see critical thought as a new dogma, a "right way" in opposition to the thoughtless people around them. As one respondent in a study done by Tey Meadow suggests, however, this is not the goal of gender fluid parenting: "I don't think parenting is having our kids grow up and making little us's. It's how do we create the safe comfortable, competent environment where they get to grow up and be themselves, whoever that is? And are there limits to that? Yes, but within a certain broad bandwidth they get to discover who they are" (737).

CONCLUSIONS

I want my children to play with gender. I want my children to be critical and authentic and to have the relative safety to name and choose their identity markers. Fostering a thoughtful response to difference, however, means understanding my mother's rage. It means understanding both why I believe my mother is wrong, that my son should get his skirt, and also her complex and convoluted reasons for being so very angry. It means teaching my children to challenge, rather than to dismiss. As Amber Kinser writes, "Every moment of mother-relating for me also is a moment of relating-in-multiplicity, of trying to reduce the friction of opposing demands of multiple selves and relationships. Survival in feminist mothering necessitates coming to see this rubbing against, this friction, this tension, not as purely oppositional and therefore needing to be resolved, but as inherent and necessary, and not in need of fixing" (124).

Teaching critical thought, teaching my children to challenge is not best done alone. I cannot model a successful critique of a neo-liberal paradigm of individualism and efficiency by keeping them to myself in order to ensure a coherent message. Instead, I have to hope that being surrounded by love and contradiction will hone their critical skills, that being forced to confront differences of opinion (some of them very painful) will give them a greater capacity for understanding. I appreciate that this response invites controversy, that in inviting dialogue rather than certainty I may expose my children to hatred, that I am privileging imperfect love over perfect safety. Yet this is all I know how to do, not following any manual, not following any sage advice, but just trusting my instincts, navigating this knife edge between where I am and where I come from and hoping that I will not fail too badly, that my best will be good enough.

WORKS CITED

Arat-Koç, Sedef. "Whose Social Reproduction? Transnational Motherhood and Challenges to Feminist Political Economy." *Social Reproduction: Feminist Political Economy Challenges Neo-Liberalism*. Eds. Kate Bezanson and Meg Luxton. Montreal: McGill-Queens University Press, 2006. 75-92. Print.

Austin, Paula. "Femme-Inism: Lessons of My Mother." *Colonize This: Young Women of Colour on Today's Feminism*. Eds. Daisy Hernández and Bushra Rehman. Emeryville, CA: Seal Press, 2002. 157-169. Print.

Baines, Donna, ed. *Doing Anti-Oppressive Practice: Social Justice Social Work*. Halifax: Fernwood Publishing, 2011. Print.

Comeau, Lisa M. "Towards White, Anti-Racist Mothering Practices: Confronting Essentialist Discourses of Race and Culture." *Journal of the Association for Research on Mothering* 9.2 (2007): 20-30. Print.

Friedman, May. *Mommyblogs and the Changing Face of Motherhood*. Toronto: University of Toronto Press, 2013.

Green, Jesse. "S/He: Why Parents of Transgender Children are Faced with a Difficult Decision." *New York Magazine* Web. 27 May, 2012.

Hernández, Daisy and Bushra Rehman, eds. *Colonize This! Young Women of Colour on Today's Feminism*. Emeryville, CA: Seal Press, 2002. Print.

Kinser, Amber E. "Mothering as Relational Consciousness." *Feminist Mothering*. Ed. Andrea O'Reilly. Albany: SUNY Press, 2008. 123-142. Print.

Kois, Dan. "Free to Be." *Slate*. Web. 22 October, 2012.

Meadow, Tey. "'Deep Down Where the Music Plays': How Parents Account for Childhood Gender Variance." *Sexualities* 14.6 (2011): 725-747. Print.

O'Reilly, Andrea, ed. *Mother outlaws: Theories and practices of empowered mothering*. Toronto: Women's Press, 2004. Print.

Shohat, Ella. *Taboo Memories, Diasporic Voices*. Durham: Duke University Press, 2006.

Tokawa, Kenji. "Why You Don't Have to Choose a White Boy Name to be a Man in this World." *Gender Outlaws: The Next Generation*. Eds. Kate Bornstein and S. Bear Bergman. Berkeley: Seal Press, 2010. Print.

Walker, Rebecca. *Black, White and Jewish: Autobiography of a Shifting Self*. New York: Riverhead Books, 2001. Print.

Weiner-Mahfuz, Lisa. "Organizing 101: A Mixed-Race Feminist in Movements for Social Justice." *Colonize This: Young Women of Colour on Today's Feminism*. Eds. Daisy Hernández and Bushra Rehman. Emeryville, CA: Seal Press, 2002. 29-39. Print.

Wilson, Shamillah, Anasuya Sengupta, and Kristy Evans, eds. *Defending Our Dreams: Global Feminist Voices for New Generation*. London: Zed Books, 2005. Print.

8.
Producing Homeplace

Strategic Sites and Liminoid Spaces
for Gender-Diverse Children

SANDRA B. SCHNEIDER

I AM LAYING POOLSIDE under an umbrella on a chaise lounge. I watch two towheaded kids sit at the edge of a municipal pool. They are presently Merpeople. Both children; my son, Benjamin a seven year-old male child and Naomi an eight year-old female child, lay back on the sun-warmed concrete surrounding the pool to kick the water as hard as possible. The water flies into the air, suspends for a fraction of a second into free-form globular shapes and then rejoins the body of water that makes up the pool.

"I am a Birl!" announces Naomi.

"A what?" asks Ben.

"A BIRL, B—irl!" Naomi states, enunciating each sound carefully.

"What is a Birl?" Ben sits up—Naomi has his full attention.

"A Birl" says Naomi "is a girl and boy—I am a Birl—a girl-boy."

"Oh," says Ben, making a connection "a broad view!" His mother uses the terms 'broad' and 'narrow' to discuss how people made sense of being a boy or girl.

"I am a Birl too!" announces Ben.

Naomi sits up pointing to her chest and then to Ben. She says in a conspiratorial tone, "We, you and I, are Birls." Ben nods affirmatively. They sit close to each other, seemingly lost in thought with their feet gently swishing back and forth in the pool.

As I reflect on my son's play, I contemplate how, as his mother, I am the primary translator and broker of my child's socialization. Children are pressured to conform to how others see them. These processes of socialization are what make children 'childish.' We patiently correct them in the proper ways to do, be, and exist.

We are amused when children 'act' like adults without honestly acknowledging what we ask children to give up.

The adult world, as American legal scholar Patricia J. Williams observed in her essay "Teleology on the Rocks," tends to ignore the unspeakable truth that conformity always requires some degree of death. Conformity, Williams reminds us, requires some abandonment of a self that can see itself and trust its own experiential knowledge. In our cultural worlds, selves develop in hierarchies and historical matrices of power that generate powerful norms. As such, non-normative selves run the risks of obliteration from powerful others who enforce and rely upon those norms. While Williams explores the intersection of identity formation and race, the intrusion of powerful norms into psyche is also acute in regards to gender and sexuality. I wonder if there will be socially acknowledged and hospitable spaces and places for Birls?

Sexuality for Michel Foucault and Richard Sennett is the "cultural medium" (1) through which adult self-consciousness emerges. For the child, it is gender: this normative intrusion consists of circumstances, responses, and experiences present in which children are made to feel 'gendered' in specific ways. As my son grows up the gender borders that progressively surround him solidify, becoming more punitive and harder for me to influence as a parent. Concerned for my son, I began to talk to other like-minded parents. I discovered that these parents very consciously support alternative 'cultural mediums' for their children; safe places to retreat, undermine stereotypes, and have experiences and spaces where their children could craft themselves. My discovery evolved into the multi-year qualitative study I share in this chapter.

INTRODUCTION

I focus on a recently concluded multi-year qualitative study in which I explored the narratives, perspectives, and parenting practices of 35 feminist parents encompassing a four-state area in the United States. Three of those states are in the Appalachian Highlands with the fourth state in the Deep South. Most of the 35 parents I interviewed reside in rural, working-class, and traditionally conservative communities.

The parents I interviewed self identify as Feminist parents, are economically diverse representing both professional and nonprofessional occupations, and represent diverse family configurations. These parents express, in practice and reflections, a commitment to the promotion of equity generally, and gender equity specifically, and acknowledge multiple oppressions both inside and outside family contexts. Living in communities where sexism and homophobia are rampant, gender diversity is a deeply cherished value and as such *gender-diverse children* means a spectrum of things to these parents; everything from transgender children to children who are gender non-conforming because they have been raised in families that reject binary notions of gender.

The parents I interviewed are committed to their children's '*gender health*.' Gender health, a term coined by Diane Ehrensaft, describes a commitment to "ensuring and facilitating an accepting and gender expansive (gender diverse) childhood that sees gender nonconformity as healthy" (21). To ensure gender health these parents consciously facilitate, acknowledge, celebrate, and value "*gender creativity*" (21): a living space where children can, with others, craft their identities. To do so, these parents construct narratives and multi-sited, connected geographies to provide safe havens for their children's exploration into their own and others' subjectivities in alternative ways and outside of the gaze of dominant culture. In this chapter I use the term children globally, whether a parent or guardian has one child or seven children. Likewise, I use the term caregiver to refer to all of the participants in my study. My goal in using caregiver is to be more inclusive and to mean any person who is the legal and day-to-day primary caregiver of a child or children.

LIVABLE LIVES: GENDER HEALTH AND AFFECTIVE PRESENCE

[My son] has two Moms, which he has had his whole life and we deal with this low-level of underlining discrimination because we live in a very rural county. (Caregiver 025, personal interviews, 06/23/2007)

Yeah I think he was afraid that if he (my son) liked those

things he would be ostracized. But I also think there is a homophobia—for my husband—absolutely. (Caregiver 019, personal interview, 01/15/2008)

Most of the caregivers I interviewed had rejected normative gender roles while their children were still infants as a natural outgrowth of their desire to provide their children with an opportunity to discover their authentic gendered self. This may be because these caregivers self-identified as feminist parents. As such, gender non-conformity was already part of the beliefs and values that were repurposed in their daily practice and sense-making of parenting and caregiving.

Many caregivers articulated their childhood experiences with sexism, homophobia, heteronormativity, and religiosity in explaining why gender-creativity and a gender-expansive childhood for their children were so important to them. As one caregiver shared:

I was twelve-years-old when my Mom caught me playing doctor with another little girl. I just knew—I knew I was gay or bi or something and she beat it out of me—she just beat it out of me. She caught me and she beat me. She held onto my little arm and beat me yelling "what is wrong with you?" When I had my son I just thought—not you, not you, you will have a choice and whoever you are is okay by me. I've got your back. Man, do I have your back! I'm Mama Wolf! (Caregiver 033, personal interview, 08/19/2010)

The caregiver articulates a relational and improvisational idea of freedom that entangles with her caring relationships and community memberships. Relationships involving care and dependency are entangled, suggesting, as Nel Noddings notes, that caring relations are "ethically basic" (3). Working from an affective stance entanglements are co-created world making.

In *Maternal Thinking* Sara Ruddick develops the deeply grounded notion of 'attentive love' (105) in which she states that Feminist or authentic caregiving "perceives and endorses a child's experience though society finds it intolerable" (105). The caregivers' ability to perceive, sacrifice to achieve, and commitment to endorse their children's need for gender health (something caregivers' themselves also require), indicates that they are 'affectively present' (Markussen 298) in their practice of care. When we are 'affectively *present*' with others we are responding within *entangled* knowledge situations. 'Present,' these caregivers perceive and give voice to the needs of their child and in turn act on the child's behalf. 'Entangled' as such, they include their children in their personal and political freedom projects, not as extensions of themselves but rather as co-journeyer with their own unique needs.

These caregivers deeply desire a good life for their children and that 'good' life, as Judith Butler discusses in *Undoing Gender*, requires that your life, your gendered expressions of who you are, is possible, recognizable, and available. Therefore, the good life requires others. That hope for a livable life is provided through homeplace. In producing homeplace caregivers create links that were not clearly established beforehand, links that modify both practices and possibilities for them and their children.

PRODUCING HOMEPLACE

> And as I went to this place I found I was really alive there, I felt really alive there and during the school year I could say—no matter how rough it is, no matter how difficult my experiences are in school, no matter how much I am struggling I will get to camp at the end of June. I have a goal—when that goal was over when I got too old, I felt really like the ground was shaking underneath me and found several other places to go in the summer that wasn't as good—well one of them was, one wasn't. It became my sanctuary and in a lot of ways remembering it is still my sanctuary. (Caregiver 025, personal interviews, 06/16/2012)

It is important to note that bell hooks uses the phrase "a site of resistance" in the title of her famous work, *Homeplace: A Site of Resistance*. Homeplace is made up of networks that include spaces, places, people, events, histories, practices, and care which offer respite and help people recuperate from a hostile normative world. In their discussion of Butler's work, human geographers Nicky

Gregson and Gillian Rose note that performativity and performance are always connected in place. Spaces and sites are performative, in that place and identity emerge through performances that occur in spaces and as such articulate power and resistance. In regards to gender health and gender creativity, homeplace for these caregivers becomes both gender-fluid places and places to dwell—places to just be, where children can craft their own gender identity.

I describe homeplace as 'multi-sited' because we live within connected geographies of places that vary in particularity and power. As Gregson and Rose state, "performance spaces are not discreet, bounded stages, but are threatened, contaminated, stained, and are enriched by other spaces" (445). Many places, like homeplaces, may be fragile but they offer spaces for the non-normative to be present or "unequally fused" (445) in the presence of power, sometimes in the form of subjectivity and memory. This means that as places leak into each other—the "messy, fuzzy, relational aspect(s) to performance" emerge (442).

I rely on the work of critical and human geographers to illustrate the spatial aspects of homeplace. In *Growing up Global*, Cindi Katz's analysis of oppositional practices and instances of resistance, Katz delineates various material social practices by using certain distinctions: resilience, reworking, and resistance (242). I use Katz's distinctions to frame caregivers' practices in producing homeplace for their children to show how these efforts build a capacity for resistance.

Resilient Acts

It was common for caregivers to develop day-to-day strategies that enable their children to be gender creative, while minimizing their risk of harm in the larger community of school, extended family, or other public places. As one caregiver stated:

> (My son) said "I really don't want to get teased so I'm not going to do that (wear a skirt) but I really want you to get me a utility kilt, a man-kilt because then I can wear it outside." I think he is looking for ways to be himself and pass at the same time. (Caregiver 025, personal interviews, 06/15/2012)

Both caregiver and child are involved in an *act of resilience* where they recognized the risks and creatively developed a solution that ensured gender creativity and, hopefully, safety.

In many instances resilient acts on behalf of their children required caregivers to rescind childcare support.

Several of the caregivers I interviewed had assumed the role of the primary caregiver or declined extended family childcare support to protect their children's gender health. As one caregiver shared:

> That's been a huge issue to be honest with you. I—the only persons that—we don't leave the children, alright…. So we haven't really left them with anybody. But we've have some real issues in terms of [Grandmother and step-Grand dad]—some real issues and we have not gotten to the point where we feel comfortable leaving the kids yet [with extended family]. (Caretaker 001, personal interview, 07/28/2007)

Fundamentally, individual resilient acts are a catalyst for, and co-evolve with, *reworking* as caregivers seek out and identify like-minded people and safe spaces for their children. As Katz states, resilient acts "enables people to get by, to enter reciprocal relations, and to shore up their resources, all of which are crucial underpinnings of projects to *rework* and resist the oppressive circumstances that call them forth" (246, emphasis mine)." 'Reworking' (247) describes an explicit acknowledgement of the problem and the deploying of practices that change the conditions of day-to-day life to enable a more livable life and to increasingly create a collective capacity for further change.

Reworking

One key aspect of Katz's notion of reworking is the ways in which "people [retool] themselves (and their children) as political subjects and social actors," (250) through what Katz refers to as 'oppositional consciousness.' Katz does not explicitly define "oppositional consciousness" (251) but other critical geographers, such as Peter Hossler have interpreted oppositional consciousness to mean "the construction of a consciousness that rejects social relation, such as capitalism or patriarchy, that produces identities that are structurally marginalized" (106). Oppositional consciousness is consciously non-normative and as such is descriptive of a disposition of critical distances from norms.

The caregivers I interviewed clearly articulated the problem at hand: binary gender norms and the subjectivity necessary to endure that problem. As one caregiver stated on learning she was pregnant with a female child:

> I was scared for her immediately. I thought, "oh no" you know I have to bring this precious girl into this world of anti-girl, anti-feminine, anti-female histories, anti-gender diverse. But I also, within 24 hours say, immediately began to think I am so glad that this young lady is coming to me when I know what I know (Caregiver 015, personal interview, 07/12/2009).

Because the caregivers themselves fight against these norms they have clear notions of how to encourage critical distance from such norms by inspiring oppositional consciousness. As one caregiver shared, she wishes to provide her daughter with a strong "sense of self. Of knowing who she is and being confident and unapologetic because I think that was the hardest thing for me" (Caregiver 018, personal interview, 06/30/2008). The ethnotheories these caregivers function within include explicitly understanding the binary gender norms and the subjectivities their children need to embody to be able to minimize internalizing *heteronormativity.*

Liminoid experiences and narratives: The making of oppositional consciousness

In making homeplace, caregivers provide self-conscious experiences not tethered to normative binary norms but rather gender creativity, and these self-conscious experiences are tactical, liminoid, and prioritize oppositional consciousness. By liminoid I mean to evoke Victor Turner's understanding of liminoid as "a place, space, and self-consciousness more freed from norms and a place to try on different subjectivities that might serve to undermine everyday life" ("Acting" 94-95). To illustrate the liminoid in homeplace I share selected examples of caregiver's tactical use of dance, daily deconstructive narratives, and personal histories. I close this section by sharing caregivers' stories of seeing their young children's critical consciousness in action.

One caregiver describes how she sought out gender-neutral (gender-free) contra dancing camps for her child to have a safe, accepting place to explore his gender expression. Contra dancing is a type of folk dance where dancers face each other in two lines and a caller, similar to square dancing, prompts the dancers. The caregiver shares her experiences with the Contra dancing community:

> Well they had one day (at the Contra dance camp) that everybody cross-dressed and he (my son) borrowed a dress or a skirt from one of the girls who was about his size, I mean they traded clothes, I think, and he really enjoyed that because he knew he enjoyed cross-dressing before that and at the dance that night one of the men came up to him and talked to him about how comfortable it is and asked him how he felt about it. And (my son) was talking about how much he really liked dancing in a skirt, he liked wearing a skirt and so the guy says "I have a present for you." And he gave (my son) a skirt someone had given him at a dance camp—years earlier that he had cut short and made a second skirt for his daughter out of it so that they matched. And he gave (my son) the skirt he'd had and that to (my son) is one of his special possessions because that went way beyond accepting and this was a man we have never seen before, we had no connection except that we were at this camp together and yet he said something to (my son) about the way (my son) was moving and the skirt or something—I don't know but he said something.... It was welcoming, it was celebrating, and it was sharing— the man was sharing something with (my son). A piece of himself—you know with a kid that is still a kid at that point. And was saying you can be straight and like doing this—it is okay because I do it and that really hit home for (my son). (Caregiver 025, personal interviews, 06/15/2012)

Contra dancing provided a place where the son could be gender creative in a community that not only acknowledged and afforded his gender expression but also celebrated and valued him. For this family, contra dancing provided an active liminoid space for gender creativity.

Victor Turner describes the liminoid as a place to be "persona in extremis" ("Acting" 94). Liminoid spaces describe "time and space betwixt and between one context of meaning and action and another"; these are messy spaces that are joined to, parallel with, and privately co-exist alongside normative public spaces (94). Liminoid places are voluntarily produced creative events, that "tend to recognize, facilitate and value individual creation, authorship, and spontaneous events and connections between people that commonly have (consciously or unconsciously) an intention to subvert dominant structures" ("Frame, Flow, Reflection" 54). These are active spaces, in the sense that the liminoid requires conscious self-creation while being bracketed off places for play, fantasy, home, alternative knowledge, the arts, and fun. These liminoid experiences provide a gender-healthy 'cultural medium' through which children become self-conscious of themselves and their world.

The caregivers I interviewed commonly deployed deconstructive narratives to critically analyze the news stories, advertisements, and mass media their children came in contact with daily. One caregiver described his family as 'constant deconstructors' to illustrate how much of a habit it was in his family. He explains: "For me, I think the most I can provide for him (my son) is a set of alternative narratives" (Caregiver 002, personal interview, 07/18/2008).

Caregivers clearly wished to develop a critical attitude toward media in their children. This is evident in that the caregivers did not always start the analysis but also encouraged their children's observations and questions about media-generated gender stereotypes. One caregiver describes a conversation with her six-year-old daughter.

The other night she (daughter) said something; she said something about a commercial on television. There was a commercial on television about a water slide and it was on one of the kids' channels and there was a commercial about a waterslide and the man came off of the water slide and he said something about "don't be embarrassed if you scream like a silly school girl." And she (my daughter) said "why did he say scream like a silly school girl, does he think there is something wrong with school girls?" And I said "fantastic question"—I try to notice when she is asking questions and opening those kinds of questions. (Caregiver 015, personal interview, 07/12/2009)

Turner states that the liminoid not only offers a number of "subjective" possibilities, but also "a *variant model for thought and action* to be accepted or rejected after careful consideration" ("Frame, Flow, Reflection" 54, emphasis mine). Private family time, conversations in cars, while watching television or looking at magazines are particular situated and embodied ways of learning. The liminoid place of family narratives of media critique makes particular kinds of critical-oriented knowing, practice, and acquisition possible.

Caregivers explicitly shared communal histories, memories, and knowledge that informed their children's broader understandings of the world and their place in that world. This caregiver explicitly addresses the erasure of intersexual people[1] in her child's formal schooling, extended family, and community at large:

He is not going to learn it in school. His grandparents who are both doctors won't tell him but he knows, and I made sure he did, that there are five sexes not two. It's not abnormal, it is different and this diversity has always been with us! (Caregiver 033, personal interview, 08/19/2010).

Caregivers also shared the history of friends and community members to teach children 'hidden histories' about discrimination in regards to gender and orientation:

I was very sad; six months ago I found out a dear friend of mine who I haven't seen in a long time had died. And she was intersexed and I had to talk about her to [my son] when it came up in some conversation about whether there were boys and girls and nothing else...so when she died that brought her up ... I told [my son] about her and told [him] about some of the struggles she had faced that I knew about because I had watched her first come out and she was raised in a good Mormon family so it was a very big deal for her. And so he—he [my son] is into people so he really thrives on these stories about how people cope and I think that is teaching him some of that resilience. (Caregiver 025, personal interviews, 06/15/2012)

These histories contribute to narratives of understanding why and how community and family members struggle with binary gender norms. As Jane Addams observed the two functions of group memories, as a reference point for individual self-reflection and a guide in selecting trajectories in social reorganization, are not mutually exclusive and most likely co-evolve as dispositions. Communal memories or histories provide a liminoid context for children's reflections on their own biography while simultaneously contextualizing caregivers' beliefs and actions and providing a critical distance regarding binary gender norms.

Caregivers' shared several stories of seeing evidence of oppositional consciousness in their young children. One caregiver shares a story about her daughter confronting normative gender roles she witnesses in her family:

We visited my sister in [Southern State] and like I said they live a very different life than we do ... and one of the things she ... does, she fixes him [her husband] supper all the time. He'll come home, put down his tray, she fixes him a plate of what she has made that includes things he likes only and put them on his plate and he leaves with his tray.... The last day she [my daughter] saw my sister making her husband food. She said "Aunt [B] why do you make Uncle [T]'s food all the time?" and (my sister) said 'because that is something I enjoy doing.' And [my daughter] said "let me tell you what I think,' and [my daughter] is six about to turn seven, "let me tell you what I think, I think Uncle [T] can get up and make his own food." And she said that to my sister, and I thought what courage and this is not like a—she's very shy; she's a quiet personality. But I thought she sees it—she sees it. (Caregiver 001, personal interview, 07/28/2007)

The caregiver states that her daughter 'sees it,' or demonstrates an ability to denaturalize her cultural gender norms. The child disregards her aunt's comment that she enjoys preparing her spouse's nightly tray and voices her judgment of her uncle's behaviour. Caregivers also shared stories that illustrated their children's comfort with gender diversity:

He's got this incredible resilience about his identity—that he can look at and be really cool with the whole thing. And with the identities of the people around him. I've seen him meet trans people and just … whatever they appear, as he just goes with it or he asks me very quietly what to call them. And then he is perfectly comfortable with it. But he notices—he notices and appreciates the difference instead of either not noticing it or being uncomfortable about it. (Caregiver 025, personal interviews, 06/15/2012)

Since homophobia is usually expressed as acute discomfort with gender diversity it is interesting to note that this caregiver connects her child's comfort with gender diversity to his resilient identity—that her son is not exhibiting homophobic discomfort. This same caregiver shares a recent conversation with her 10 year-old son regarding his sexual orientation.

He came up to me one day … and said "Mommy I'm bi" and I said "okay—you probably don't want to tell your friends yet, I am not sure they would understand." And he was like "okay." He was so matter-of-fact about it. That was the coolest thing … the matter-of-factness was what really made me feel like I had done my job right—because he wasn't coming to me shy, he wasn't embarrassed, he wasn't uncomfortable. (Caregiver 025, personal interviews, 06/15/2012)

Her son's 'matter-of-factness' indicates to this caregiver that she had "done her job well"—her son embraces his fluid gender and sexual orientations without emotional conflict or discomfort. These children demonstrate dispositions of oppositional consciousness where they reject binary gender norms as they come in contact with them. Both of these children engage, on a similar scale, in behaviours and sense-making that conflicts with the binary gender norms they encounter without feeling the emotional discomfort of calling their own identities into question. These children possess identities that are congruent with their actions as they craft themselves as gender-diverse beings and come in contact with various normative expectations. Contemplation of their gender, identity and self is not 'a problem' but a source of resiliency.

CONCLUSION

Katz sees resilient acts, reworking, and oppositional consciousness as important ways communities build a capacity for *resistance*. The everyday acts these caregivers engage in redress the imposition of hegemonic norms and involve nurturing children's long-term oppositional consciousness. In Judith Butler's discussion of autonomy she states that adults "have other discourses available for understanding who they are and want to be" (82). This is precisely what young children do not have at their disposal.

Young children are in the process of acquiring their culture to function and acquiring the embodied habits that will differentiate them to be specific adult actors. In working toward new understandings of child empowerment, as Gregson and Rose note we must make deeper connections between embodiment, performing bodies, and the performative. My hope in sharing this study is that the examination of sites of reworking for young children may yield additional support for alternative spatial-temporal-liminoid views of empowerment and resilience rather than the prevailing individual, atomistic, one-event views of empowerment.

[1]Caregiver 033 clarified that she was familiar with Dr. Anne Fausto-Sterling's article entitled "The Five Sexes." In the article

Fausto-Sterling, intending to be provocative and inclusive, suggests a notion of gender containing five sexes: male, female, merm, ferm, and herm. The erasure this caregiver was conveying was that of intersexual people.

WORKS CITED

Addams, Jane. *The Long Road of Woman's Memory*. Chicago: University of Illinois Press, 1916/2002. Print.

Butler, Judith. *Undoing Gender.* New York: Routledge, 2004. Print.

Ehrensaft, Diane. *Gender Born, Gender Made: Raising Healthy Gender-Nonconforming Children*. New York: The Experiment, LLC, 2011. Print.

Fausto-Sterling, A. "The Five Sexes: Why Male and Female Are Not Enough." *The Sciences* (March/April 1993): 20–24. Print.

Foucault, Michel and Richard Sennett, "Sexuality and Solitude." *Humanities in Review, Volume 1*. Eds. Ronald Dworkin, Karl Miller, and Richard Sennett. London: The New York Institute for the Humanities/ Cambridge University Press, 1982. 3-21. Print.

Gregson, Nicky and Gillian Rose. "Taking Butler Elsewhere: Performativities, Spatialities and Subjectivities." *Environment and Planning D: Society and Space*. 18 (2000): 433-452. Print.

hooks, bell. "Homeplace: a Site of Resistance." 1990. *Maternal Theory*. Ed. Andrea O'Reilly. Bradford: Demeter Press, 2007. 382-390. Print.

Hossler, Peter. "Free Health Clinics, Resistance and the Entanglement of Christianity and Commodified Health Care Delivery." *Antipode* 44.1 (2012): 98-121. Print.

Katz, Cindi. *Growing up Global: Economic Restructuring and Children's Everyday Lives*. Minneapolis: University of Minnesota Press, 2004. Print.

Markussen, Turid. "The Performativity of Affective Engagement." *Feminist Theory* 7.3 (2006): 291-308. Print.

Noddings, Nel. *Starting at Home: Caring and Social Policy*. Berkeley: University of California Press, 2002. Print.

Ruddick, Sara. *Maternal Thinking: Toward a Politics of Peace*. 1989. Boston, MA: Beacon Press, 1995. Print.

Turner, Victor. "Acting in Everyday Life and Everyday Life in

Acting." *Humanities in Review. Volume 1*. Eds. Ronald Dwor-kin, Karl Miller, and Richard Sennett. London: The New York Institute for the Humanities/Cambridge University Press, 1982. 83-105. Print.

Turner, Victor. "Frame, Flow and Reflection: Ritual and Drama as Public Liminality." *Performance in Postmodern Culture*. Eds. Michel Benamou and Charles Caramello. Madison, WI: Coda Press.1977. 33- 55. Print.

Williams, Patricia J. "Teleology on the Rocks." *The Alchemy of Race and Rights: Diary of a Law Professor*. Cambridge: Harvard University Press, 1992. Print.

9.
Complicating the Truth of Gender

Gender Literacy and the Possible Worlds of Trans Parenting

JAKE PYNE

WITHIN PHILOSOPHICAL THOUGHT, the term *a priori knowledge* is understood as knowledge that we hold by virtue of reason alone, something that we need not find out. The statement "all fathers are male" is commonly used as an example of *a priori* knowledge, a statement that is thought to be "true in all possible worlds" (Russell). It is safe to say that transgender (trans) parents complicate this truth.

This chapter reports on the findings of a community-based research project called *Transforming Family* in Toronto, Canada. Primarily focused on trans parent's experiences of discrimination, this project also set out to document the strengths that trans people bring to parenting—as Rachel Epstein notes, strengths they bring because of, rather than in spite of, their experiences as trans people (30). This chapter highlights one strength in particular: *complicating the truth of gender*, at times a purposeful undertaking by participants, other times the inadvertent effect of their simply existing. Trans parents in this study preserved gender options for their children, expanded notions of biological possibilities, negotiated new identities, and role modeled authenticity and embodiment. With and without intention, trans people who are parents complicate the truth of gender and open up possibilities for raising gender literate kids.

WILL THE KIDS BE ALRIGHT? RESEARCH ABOUT
TRANS PARENTS AND THEIR CHILDREN

In the public imaginary, trans people are often the stuff of daytime talk shows—outlandish and extraordinary in every way. Juxtaposed against the often mundane tasks of family life, trans people and parenting are unlikely companions. Yet recent Canadian and U.S. surveys have found that, respectively, 27 percent (Bauer et al. "Trans People in Ontario") and 38 percent (Grant et al.) of trans people are parents (88). Trans people are most certainly raising children. In the limited literature that addresses trans parents, however, their adequacy has often been called into question.

In the early texts that accompanied the North American gender identity clinics of the 1960s,[1] parents pursuing a gender transition were discouraged from seeking child custody and were advised instead to sever or suspend relationships with their children (Brown and Rounsley 187). For a child to no longer have one of their parents was seen as potentially preferable to having a trans parent. Richard Green and John Money wrote: "Young children are better told that their parents are divorcing and that daddy will be living far away and unable to see them" (287). Betty Steiner echoed these doubts in another clinical text as she wondered dramatically about trans men's suitability for fatherhood: "...What does the future hold for this baby whose father is a penisless man?" (cited in Lev 312). Steiner chose not to elabourate on which parenting tasks, in her view, require a penis, prompting Arlene Lev to later remark that preoccupation with the welfare of trans people's children has at times "bordered on the absurd" (312).

Empirical studies exploring wellbeing among the children of trans parents have yet to find any evidence that having a transgender parent will, in and of itself, negatively affect a child (Freedman, Tasker and di Ceglie 423; Green "Sexual Identity," "Transsexuals Children"; White and Ettner "Adaptation and Adjustment," "Disclosure"). Researchers and clinicians have instead found multiple factors which determine children's wellbeing during a parent's gender transition: the quality of family relationships (Freedman, Tasker and di Ceglie 423); information sharing and communication (Harris 168; Hines 364); children's age (Raj 140); and parental conflict (White and Ettner "Disclosure"). Yet doubts about the acceptability of trans parents resurface in fertility and bioethics literature where clinicians debate whether it is ethical to assist trans people to become parents (Baetens, Camus, and Devroey;

Brothers and Ford; Jones; Mishra). Lance Wahlert and Autumn Fiester note that the debates about trans peoples' right to assisted reproduction reflect the scrutiny and "suspicious gaze" directed at trans people in general (283). Paul De Sutter points out that these debates are profoundly insulting (612).

Arguably, at the heart of the unease with trans parents is a concern regarding whether trans people will make good "gender role models" for children (Hicks "Gender Role Models"). Indeed studies have investigated whether trans parents will disproportionately raise gay or trans children (Cameron; Green, "Sexual Identity," "Transsexuals Children"; Freedman, Tasker and Di Ceglie). These studies have largely concluded that the children of trans parents will grow up to be cisgender (non-trans) heterosexuals,[2] and therefore in Richard Green's words "do not differ" from children raised in conventional families ("Sexual Identity" 696-697). Curiously, this assumes that all children raised by cisgender heterosexuals will grow up to be cisgender heterosexuals themselves. Given that most lesbian, gay, bisexual and transgender (LGBT) people *were* raised in families that could be called "conventional," this is clearly not the case.

Regardless of whether or not "sameness" can be said to exist between trans and non-trans parents, the appeal to it is of interest and mirrors the tendency within research to downplay the differences between the children of same-sex parents versus those of heterosexual parents. Judith Stacey and Timothy Biblarz re-evaluated 21 studies about same-sex parenting, finding that differences among the children were much more common than were reported. One of the differences found was that the children of same-sex parents conformed less to gender stereotypes and their parents were less concerned that they exhibit gender-typical behaviours (168, 172). Yet in original study findings, it was most often reported that no significant difference had been found (170). Stacey and Biblarz acknowledge the historical context of this omission: a fear that any differences would be interpreted as deficits at a time when gay and lesbian parents were fighting for custody of their children in courts (170). Epstein notes that Stacey and Biblarz's exploration of difference marks a shift away from defensiveness and towards curiosity, made possible by the social and legal recognition that some gay and lesbian parents have achieved (16).

The context of fear that marked research with gay and lesbian parents extends to trans parents as well. Severe bias against trans parents has been well documented in U.S. family courts (Chang; Flynn; Green "Parental Alienation"; Minter; Tye) and substantial barriers to maintaining child custody and access have been documented for trans parents in Canada (Pyne 14). Yet we are also witnessing a new exploration of uniqueness in trans parenting. Sally Hines describes the reciprocal care evident between the trans parents and children in her study (365). The children of trans parents in Abigail Garner's (34) study and in Monica Canfield-Lenfest's (22) resource manual describe learning open-mindedness and the importance of social critique. With respect to gender roles, Maura Ryan notes that the lack of existing social scripts for trans fathers, may uniquely free them to challenge patriarchal fatherhood (149). Abbie Goldberg notes the intriguing questions arising from this gendering and de-gendering of parenting (84). While asserting that trans parents are no different from others may be necessary in some contexts, this also forecloses discussion of those differences that might be strengths. Though there is a risk of simplifying trans parent's lives by focusing on their strengths alone, the question has been so neglected, it begs exploration.

THE TRANSFORMING FAMILY PROJECT: TRANS VOICES ON PARENTING

The *Transforming Family* project was a community-based qualitative study exploring the impact of transphobia on trans people who are parents as well as their perceptions of their parenting strengths. Led by a trans parent, the project was a collabouration between the LGBTQ Parenting Network at the Sherbourne Health Centre and the Researching for LGBTQ Health team at the Centre for Addiction and Mental Health (CAMH) in Toronto. The goal of this project was to help trans parents articulate their experiences and to better position them to respond to the policies and practices impacting their families.

In November 2010, four focus groups were held with a total of eighteen trans parents. Eligibility included identifying as trans, identifying as a parent and living in the Toronto area or nearby. Two focus groups (five people in each group) included participants who were parents before coming out as trans or transitioning, all of whom were trans women (male-to-female). A third focus group was made up of those who had become parents after transitioning, including one trans woman and two trans men. A fourth focus group included a mixture of five individuals who had been parents before identifying as trans, as well as those who had become parents after identifying as trans. All five of these individuals were on the female-to-male spectrum, several of them identified as gender queer.[3] Focus group questions related to discrimination, strategies for resisting discrimination and participants' perceptions of their parenting strengths. Focus groups were recorded and transcribed and the analysis (using a grounded theory method) was conducted by three trans researchers. Participants identified a number of strengths; this chapter focuses on one strength in particular—the ability to complicate the truth of gender.

THE TRUTH ABOUT GENDER

One need not look far for the dominant view of gender: there are two distinct and easily distinguishable sexes, immutable and stable over time; the relationship between sex and gender is mechanical, with gender as the natural expression, the social mirror, of biological sex (Stryker 9). As Viviane Namaste notes, the very existence of trans people has been rendered impossible (4-5). As Greta Bauer et al. point out, the assumption that everyone born male will become a man, and that everyone born female will become a woman, is so pervasive it is rarely spoken ("Erasure" 356).

The field of child development makes an interesting study of how modern gender truth is produced. It is often noted that small children tend to hold open the possibility that their own gender, or that of others, might change (Berk 539; Bukatko and Daehler 460; Puckett and Black 273). But rather than regard this as a capacity, it is framed in child development as a cognitive limitation: "Slowly they [preschoolers] comprehend that they cannot change their sex no matter what they do" (Steinberg and Belsky 281). Acceptance of this "fact" is referred to as the developmental milestone of *gender stability* (the "knowledge" that gender cannot change) or *gender constancy* (the "knowledge" that changing one's appearance does not change one's gender) (Bukatko and Daehler 460). *Gender constancy*, in fact, is said to indicate the ability to distinguish reality from fiction (Berk 539). While child development literature has been influenced by feminist and queer movements and most certainly challenges gender stereotypes (Bee 237), the notion that constancy and stability are the truth of gender, remains largely undebated.

Yet this normative view of gender has not gone unchallenged. Early social scientists (Garfinkle) and feminist researchers (Kessler and McKenna) laid the foundation for framing gender as a social construct, as something that we *do*, rather than as a natural property. Post-structural thought and the queer and feminist theories that have stemmed from it have emphasized the fluidity and performativity of gender as well as its imitative and discursive structure (Butler). Indeed, some have called for an "end" to gender (Brudge) and even asked "do we really need it at all?" (Hicks "Gender Role Models" 52). As Lauren Bialystock notes, the claim that there can be nothing essential or authentic about gender has become de rigueur within many streams of feminism. Yet as trans and non-trans scholars have argued, this alternate truth has had the unfortunate effect of legitimizing some narratives (queer and transgender) while delegitimizing others, namely those of transsexuals who have been cast as rigid and conservative for claiming an authentic self and taking medical steps to live in accordance with that self (Bialystock; Elliot; Prosser; Rubin). It is important to note then, that trans people broadly, and these trans parents in particular, may challenge both the modern truth of gender and the post-modern one as well. This chapter explores the way in which they do so.

"SUCH A GOOD FOUNDATION": PRESERVING GENDER OPTIONS

As Emily Kane notes, many parents guide their children into gender norms out of a commitment to heteronormativity or a sense of accountability to others (149). Yet participants who were raising young children described efforts to avoid over-determining gender. A trans man, Ishai (a pseudonym), recalls:

132

I was walking with the dog and the baby, and a woman asked: "Boy or a girl?" so I said: "And which one of us are you referring to?"

Parents recounted stories of allowing their children to explore clothing and activities typically reserved for the other gender. Josh, a trans man recalls playing with his son:

There were high-heeled shoes and he asked what they were and he wanted to put them on. The older boy said "oh no, those aren't for boys" and I walked over and said "I'll help you put them on ... they're hard to walk in but you can try and I'll hold your hand."

These strategies could arguably be said to be rooted in feminist parenting practices rather than reflecting a uniquely trans perspective on parenting. Yet some of participant's practices also went beyond the goal of challenging stereotypes. Josh described how he responded to questions about his newborn child: "I'd say 'yeah it's a boy, but you know, that can change'." The message that gender can change is not typically conveyed even within progressive parenting communities, yet participants themselves were split regarding whether they felt their parenting approaches were unique to them as trans people or whether they might share these approaches with other parents. Dunya, a gender queer parent said: "I definitely don't think that would happen if I wasn't my gender queer self." However, Josh stated: "I can imagine a cisgender person who is trans-aware making all the same choices."

As parents, participants reflected on their own challenging childhood experiences, attempting to offer something better to their children. Kelly, a trans woman, said:

I didn't see the variety of identities ... and that made it really hard for me to understand who I was and to find myself in the world. He won't have that problem, because he'll have been exposed to so much ... it won't be as hard for him to claim his own identity.

Gender queer parent Alfred stated:

> She [my daughter] is quite clear that she's a girl, but ... she
> is exploring things that are non-traditionally girl attributes
> ... a wider range of possibility, certainly than I experienced
> as a child ... and that will extend through her life in such
> a good way, it's such a good foundation.

When considering what these options are a good foundation
for, Alfred spoke of his daughters' unique ability to grasp gender
possibilities, dubbing this skill "gender literacy":

> The youngest child in our family is extremely, I would
> say, "gender literate."...She navigates our world very
> comfortably.

"A LOT MORE THINGS ARE POSSIBLE THAN PEOPLE WILL LET YOU THINK": EXPANDING BIOLOGICAL POSSIBILITIES

In 2008, in a brief article in *The Advocate*, trans man Thomas
Beatie launched himself into international fame as what many
called the "first pregnant man." Though trans communities were
adamant that Beatie was not the first, Ryan notes that Beatie
created the first public space for the concept of pregnant men
(139). Several participants in this study also came to be parents
in ways that challenged scientific notions of the "possible." Like
Beatie, trans man Ishai had a child through his own pregnancy
and recalled the ways that others were compelled to reckon with
this new reality. For example, after considerable advocacy, the
Office of the Registrar General issued Ishai and his partner one of
the first Ontario birth certificates with no mother listed, featuring
instead one "father" and one "father/other parent." Ishai recalls
what made this possible:

> It took us standing in the office with a newborn baby, look-
> ing like a couple of exhausted bearded guys waving around
> the Ontario Human Rights Policy on Gender Identity, like,
> literally waving around the long version of their policy.

Samantha, a trans woman, also came to motherhood through unique means: by storing sperm samples prior to her transition, she was able to later conceive a child with her female partner. Samantha's experience involved many struggles to be recognized as a mother by fertility clinic staff, midwives, birth coaches, family members, and the Ontario Birth Registration system. Yet Samantha found her own ways to acknowledge multiple possibilities as she raised her young son:

> Instead of teaching him that boys have penises and girls have vaginas, we just say *most* boys have penises and *most* girls have vaginas, and so that teaches him a general pattern while allowing for exceptions.

An insider knowledge of being one such "exception" is one of the things trans parents offer. Josh recalled his mother's reaction when he announced his plans to have a child with his partner: "Mom said: 'Oh well how are you gonna do that!?!'" In a focus group consisting entirely of trans parents, Josh's story was met with raucous laughter. As trans woman Jacquelin notes, one of the things trans parents teach, is that "A lot more things are possible, than people will let you think."

"MY SISTER IS YOUR UNCLE": NEGOTIATING NEW IDENTITIES

An additional possibility that trans parents open up is the potential for new identities beyond man or woman, mother or father. Dunya, for example, a gender queer participant who was pregnant at the time of the focus group, informed the group that they[4] were planning to refer to themselves as a "mapa": part mama, part papa. Another gender queer participant on the female-to-male spectrum, Judy, was comfortable using "she" but chose to adopt the title "dad" when she became a parent, as she felt this best described her role. Judy recounted the interesting conversations that have resulted:

> The kids will say: 'Why are you his dad?' because I also use "she" ... and I get this great opportunity to say: 'Yeah, do you know anyone else like me in your life? Anyone whose

gender isn't all one way?' It's a really great effect that I get to have that I feel really good about.

Judy went on to describe another naming practice that brings her distinct identity into view:

> With my younger nephew ... his father, my brother, said to him: "You know, my sister is your uncle" ... and he's just got that as a part of his world. It's so cool to have these opportunities to be seen.

Judy points out two simultaneous benefits to this blurring of gender lines: that her nephew has a broad perspective on gender as "a part of his world" and that she herself is able to be "seen." In fact, Judy notes that her child has begun to experiment with calling her "he," yet she feels that the coherence that "he" accomplishes together with "dad," erases a unique identity that she prefers to be visible.

> [Child's name] has a little bit lately started trying out calling me "he," which is just fascinating to me. On some level, I don't like it, because I love how quickly I am saying something more true about myself when I say "dad" and "she" in the same sentence.

For other participants, this blurring of gender lines was not necessarily their wish. For example, when participants had children before identifying as trans or transitioning, their children typically had established relationships with them as either a mother or a father. In most cases, those roles were not interchangeable in the child's view, and they sometimes chose not to change how they referred to that parent. For a trans woman called Kelly, this resulted in her also being both "dad" and "she":

> For a while I encouraged him [my son] to try to pick something different than "dad" so he wouldn't 'out' me all the time, and he refused ... I said "alright I'll be dad" ... So my gender changed but he didn't have to give up on

having his father, he just has a father who is female. He uses female pronouns, calls me dad, that's fine.

Other children of transitioning parents chose to abandon "mom" and "dad" altogether. Elliot, a trans man with adult children, re-counts some of his son's amusing new terms, along with his own hesitation:

He's [my son] come up with maddy: half mommy half dad. Or, manmom, which is funnier, I kinda don't mind man-mom [laughter] or manly mom is even better! [laughter] but it's not really what you want in the kind of ordinary moment, and it's not particularly what you want in public.

Thus some participants did not set out to shake the foundations of gender, yet they still offer a challenge to the *a priori* assumption that fathers are always men and mothers are always women. As female fathers, maddies, man-moms and mapas, they offer us a glimpse of the possible worlds of gender.

"TRUE IS WHAT *YOU* SAY": ROLE MODELING EMBODIMENT

Though many parents recounted stories of playing with gender, this did not mean that gender was unimportant to them. Indeed, one of the messages participants conveyed to their children was the importance of embodying the gendered self. Embodiment, the way bodies shape and are shaped by social practices, is increasingly a feature of gender theory. As Raewyn Connell notes, all genders are embodied, and all are embodied with contradictions, though for trans people, both the scope of that contradiction and its remedy can be extensive (867).

While transsexual transition has often been cast as a form of mutilation, a departure from the self, as Jay Prosser counters, transition should be understood as a return to an integrated self—a journey home (83). Through example, trans parents in this study emphasized to their children the importance of facing the world as their authentic self, as that self is felt and known. Jane recalled:

My oldest one, I remember her saying several months into it my transition that she realized she'd never seen me really laugh up until then ... fifteen years of her life and she had never seen me laugh or smile. She came up and said: "I can see that you're happier now."

Similarly, Tracey's daughter seemed to understand the importance of embodiment through witnessing a moment of its opposite. Tracey transitioned from male to female when her daughter was in the difficult years of middle school. At her daughter's request, Tracey agreed to present herself as male for her daughter's grade eight graduation. Yet Tracey describes her daughter's reaction upon seeing her:

I said "So how do you want me to present when I come?" and she said "as a boy." And I said "okay" ... but the first thing that came out of her mouth when she saw me was "I'm sorry."

When asked what they offered their children, specifically as trans people, participants reiterated the gift of authenticity. Trans woman Jacquelin reflected: "One of the lessons we teach, is that true is not what other people say, true is what *you* say." As stated, these lessons were not necessarily intentional, but the effect of witnessing a parent make a profound life change in pursuit of wholeness and wellbeing. Trans woman Lisa said of her son: "The thing I taught him, without actually teaching it to him, is courage."

DISCUSSION

Stephen Hicks points out that the question of whether LGBT parents can be good "gender role models" has been used to cast them as poor candidates for parenting ("Question of Gender," 150). Hicks maintains that to have a "gender role model" at all, is not actually a child development need, but simply a reproduction of stable gender norms ("Gender Role Models" 43). Setting aside the debate as to whether role models are needed, it is clear that if trans parents are role modeling anything, it is something distinct and valuable. While the field of child development calls for children to learn gender as *stability* and *constancy*, these parents taught gender *complexity*. Though to imagine gender possibilities is thought to be a cognitive limitation (Bukatko and Daehler 460), these parents understood this as a "literacy" skill, needed not only for forming one's own identity, but for reading the identities of others in a complex social world. Though the notion of authenticity is rejected by many queer and feminist theorists, participants conveyed what is for many, the fundamental importance of the gendered self and of facing the world as that self.

In closing, the trans parents in the *Transforming Family* study offered unique gifts to their children. As Rachel Epstein notes, this was not in spite of, but because of, who they were (30). With and without intention, participants preserved gender options for their children; they expanded biological possibilities; they negotiated new identities; and they role modeled authenticity and embodiment. In so doing, these and other trans parents are complicating the truth of gender, opening up the possibility of a new gender literate generation and offering us a glimpse of other possible worlds.

The author would like to thank the eighteen research participants, in addition to Rachel Epstein, Lori Ross, Scott Anderson and Kinnon MacKinnon for their guidance and assistance with this study.

[1] Gender Identity Clinics first emerged in the 1960's in North America to assess and determine the eligibility of those desiring sex-change procedures (Meyerowitz 133).

[2] The exception was Cameron's (2006) study, the results of which are evident in the title of his article: "Children of homosexuals and transsexuals more apt to be homosexual" in which he argues that LGBTQ people should not be permitted to parent children, on this basis. Cameron's research methods consisted of reading three anthologies of the writings of children of LGBTQ parents retrieved from Amazon.com. His work was quickly criticized as unsound (Morrison, 2007).

[3] Gender queer refers to those who identify their gender outside

of traditional categories, not necessarily as either trans men or trans women.

[4]This participant uses the gender-neutral pronoun 'they' rather than 'he' or 'she'.

WORKS CITED

Baetens, Patricia, M. Camus, and P. Devroey. "Should Requests for Donor Insemination on Social Grounds be Expanded to Transsexuals?" *Reproductive BioMedicine Online* 6.3 (2003): 281. Print.

Bauer, G., Michelle Boyce, Todd Coleman, Matt Kaay and Kyle Scanlon. "Who Are Trans People in Ontario?" *Trans PULSE E-Bulletin* 1.1 (2010): 1-2. Print.

Bauer, G., Rebecca Hammond, Robb Travers, Matt Kaay, Karen Hohenadel and Michelle Boyce. "'I Don't Think This Is Theoretical; This Is Our Lives': How Erasure Impacts Health Care for Transgender People." *Journal of the Association of Nurses in AIDS Care* 20.5 (2009): 348-361. Print.

Beatie, Thomas. "Labour of Love." *Advocate*. Web. March 26, 2008.

Bee, Helen. *The Growing Child*. New York. Harper Collins Publishers, 1995. Print.

Berk, Laura. *Child Development*. Boston, MA: Pearson Education, 2006. Print.

Bialystock, Lauren. "Authenticity and Trans Identity." *Talk About Sex: A Multidisciplinary Discussion*. Ed. Robert Scott Stewart. Sydney, NS: Cape Breton University Press, 2013. Print.

Brothers, Di, and W. C. L. Ford. "Gender Reassignment and Assisted Reproduction: An Ethical Analysis." *Human Reproduction* 15.4 (2000): 737-738. Print.

Brown, Mildred and Chloe Ann Rounsley. *True Selves: Understanding Transsexualism—For Families, Friends, Coworkers, and Helping Professionals*. San Francisco: Jossey-Bass Publishers, 1996. Print.

Brudge, Barbara. "Bending Gender, Ending Gender: Theoretical Foundations for Social Work Practice with the Transgender Community." *Social Work* 52.3 (2007): 243-250. Print.

Bukatko, Danuta and Marvin Daehler. *Child Development: A Thematic Approach*. Boston, MA: Houghton-Mifflin Company, 2001. Print.

Butler, Judith. *Gender Trouble*. New York: Routledge, 1999. Print.

Cameron, Paul. "Children of Homosexuals and Transsexuals More Apt to be Homosexual." *Journal of Biosocial Science* 38.3 (2006): 413-418. Print.

Canfield-Lenfest, Monica. *Kids of Trans Resource Guide*. San Francisco: COLAGE, 2008. Print.

Chang, Helen. "My Father is a Woman, Oh No!: The Failure of the Courts to Uphold Individual Substantive Due Process Rights for Transgender Parents Under the Guise of the Best Interest of the Child." *Santa Clara Law Review* 43 (2003): 649. Print.

Connell, Raewyn. "Transsexual Women and Feminist Thought: Toward New Understanding and New Politics." *Signs* 37.4 (2012): 857-881. Print.

De Sutter, Paul. "Gender Reassignment and Assisted Reproduction: Present and Future Reproductive Options for Transsexual People." *Human Reproduction* 16.4 (2009): 612-614. Print.

Elliot, Patricia. *Debates in Transgender, Queer, and Feminist Theory: Contested Sites*. Surrey, UK: Ashgate Publishing, 2010. Print.

Epstein, Rachel. *Who's Your Daddy? And Other Writings on Queer Parenting*. Toronto: Sumach Press, 2009. Print.

Flynn, Taylor. "The Ties That (Don't) Bind: Transgender Family Law and the Unmaking of Families." *Transgender Rights*. Eds. Paisley Currah, Richard Juang and Shannon Minter, Minneapolis: University of Minnesota Press, 2006. 32-50. Print.

Freedman, David, Fiona Tasker, and Domenico di Ceglie. "Children and Adolescents with Transsexual Parents Referred to a Specialist Gender Identity Development Service: A Brief Report of Key Developmental Features." *Clinical Child Psychology and Psychiatry* 7.3 (2002): 423-432. Print.

Garfinkle, Harold. "Passing and the Managed Achievement of Sex Status in an 'Intersexed' Person." *The Transgender Studies Reader*. Eds. Susan Stryker and Stephen Whittle. New York: Routledge, 2006. 656-666. Print.

Garner, Abigail. *Families Like Mine: Children of Gay Parents Tell*

It Like It Is. New York: Harper Collins Publishers, 2004. Print.

Goldberg, Abbie. *Lesbian and Gay Parents and Their Children: Research on the Family Life Cycle.* Washington, DC: American Psychological Association, 2010. Print.

Grant, Jamie, Lisa Mottet, Justin Tanis, Jack Harrison, Jody Herman and Mara Keisling. *Injustice at Every Turn: A Report of the National Transgender Discrimination Survey.* Washington, DC: National Center for Transgender Equality and National Gay and Lesbian Task Force, 2011. Print.

Green, Richard. "Sexual Identity of 37 Children Raised by Homosexual or Transsexual Parents." *The American Journal of Psychiatry* 135.6 (1978): 692-697. Print.

Green, Richard. "Transsexuals Children."*International Journal of Transgenderism* 2.4 (1998). Print.

Green, Richard. "Parental Alienation Syndrome and the Transsexual Parent." *International Journal of Transgenderism* 9.1 (2006): 9-13. Print.

Green, Richard and John Money. *Transsexualism and Sex Reassignment.* Baltimore: John Hopkins Press, 1969. Print.

Harris, Martha. "Issues for Transgenders in Therapy." *Trans Forming Families: Real Stories About Transgendered Loved Ones.* Ed. Mary Boenke, Hardy, VA: Oak Knoll Press, 2003. 159-161. Print.

Hicks, Stephen. "Gender Role Models … Who Needs 'Em?" *Qualitative Social Work* 7.1 (2008): 43–59. Print.

Hicks, Stephen. "Lesbian, Gay, Bisexual, and Transgender Parents and the Question of Gender." *LGBT-Parent Families: Innovations in Research and Implications for Practice.* Eds. Abbie Goldberg and Katherine Allen. New York: Springer Press, 2013. 149-162. Print.

Hines, Sally. Intimate Transitions: Transgender Practices of Partnering and Parenting. *Sociology* 40.2 (2006): 353-371. Print.

Jones, Howard. "Gender Reassignment and Assisted Reproduction: Evaluation of Multiple Aspects." *Human Reproduction* 15.5 (2000): 987. Print.

Kane, Emily. "No Way My Boys Are Going To Be Like That: Parents Responses to Gender Non-Conformity." *Gender and Society* 20 (2006): 149-176. Print.

Kessler, Susan and Wendy McKenna. "Toward a Theory of Gender." *The Transgender Studies Reader.* Eds. Susan Stryker and Stephen Whittle. New York: Routledge, 2006. 656-666. Print.

Lev, Arlene Istar. *Transgender Emergence: Therapeutic Guidelines for Working with Gender Variant People and Their Families.* New York: Haworth Clinical Practice Press, 2004. Print.

Meyerowitz, Joanne. *How Sex Changed: A History of Transsexuality in the United States.* Cambridge: Harvard University Press, 2002. Print.

Minter, Shannon. *A Legal Guide to Child Custody and Selected Family Law Issues for Transsexual and Transgendered Parents.* San Francisco: National Center for Lesbian Rights, 1998. Print.

Mishra, Ruchika. "The Case: IVF Treatment for an HIV-Discordant Transgender Couple?" *Cambridge Quarterly of Healthcare Ethics* 21.2 (2012): 281. Print.

Morrison, Todd. "Children of Homosexuals and Transsexuals More Apt to be Homosexual: A Reply to Cameron." *Journal of Biosocial Science* 39.1 (2007): 153-154.

Namaste, Viviane. *Invisible Lives: The Erasure Of Transsexual And Transgendered People.* Chicago: University of Chicago Press, 2000. Print.

Prosser, Jay. *Second Skins: The Body Narratives of Transsexuality.* New York: Columbia University Press, 1998. Print.

Puckett, Margaret and Janet Black. *The Young Child: Development from Prebirth through Age Eight.* York, PA: McGraw-Hill, 2005. Print.

Pyne, Jake. *Transforming Family: Trans Parents and their Struggles, Strategies, and Strengths.* Toronto: LGBTQ Parenting Network, 2012. Print.

Raj, Rupert. "Transforming Couples and Families: A Trans-Formative Therapeutic Model for Working with the Loved-Ones of Gender-Divergent Youth and Trans-Identified Adults." *Journal of GLBT Family Studies* 4.2 (2008): 133-163.

Rubin, Henry. "Phenomenology as Method in Trans Studies." *GLQ* 4.2. (1998): 263-281.

Russell, Bruce, *A Priori Justification and Knowledge. The Stanford Encyclopedia of Philosophy.* 2012. Web. 8 January 2013.

Ryan, Maura. "Beyond Thomas Beatie: Trans Men and the New

Parenthood." *Who's Your Daddy? And Other Writings on Queer Parenting*. Ed. Rachel Epstein. Toronto: Sumach Press, 2009. 139-150. Print.

Stacey, Judith and Timothy Biblarz. "(How) Does the Sexual Orientation of Parents Matter?" *American Sociological Review* 66.2 (2001) 159-183. Print.

Steinberg, Laurence and Jay Belsky. *Infancy, Childhood and Adolescence: Development in Context*. New York: McGraw-Hill, 1991. Print.

Tye, Marcus C. "Lesbian, Gay, Bisexual, and Transgender Parents: Special Considerations for the Custody and Adoption Evaluator." *Family Court Review, Special Issue: Troxel v. Granville and its Implications for Families and Practice: A Multidisciplinary Symposium* 41.1 (2003): 92-103. Print.

Wahlert, Lance and Autumn Fiester. "Commentary: The Questions We Shouldn't Ask." *Cambridge Quarterly of Healthcare Ethics* 21.2 (2012): 282-284. Print.

White, T. and R. Ettner. "Disclosure, Risks and Protective Factors for Children Whose Parents are Undergoing a Gender Transition." *Journal of Gay and Lesbian Psychotherapy* 8.1 (2004): 129-145. Print.

White, T. and R. Ettner. "Adaptation and Adjustment in Children of Transsexual Parents." *European Child and Adolescent Psychiatry* 16.4 (2007): 215-221. Print.

10.
Pink Butterflies and Blue Caterpillars

ARWEN BRENNEMAN

I N EARLY 2002, my first baby was born. I held the beautiful little person to me, smiling into his grey-eyed and serious face, and realized our list of boys' names wasn't going to work; they were afterthought names, not serious choices. Without really realizing it, we'd assumed we were having a girl. A series of small events had coloured our view, starting with our routine ultrasound: we hadn't asked the sex because we didn't have a preference, but we were pretty sure the ultrasound technician had slipped and said 'she.' Later, my husband woke from a dream of a daughter with wide dark eyes. It was easy for me to imagine because I'd grown up surrounded by girls.

We first started talking about parenting and gender when shopping for baby things. Pink was everywhere! Wandering in a department store, we played a grown up hide and seek: the winner would be the parent with the most items for a girl that did not contain pink. Eventually, we joined forces, because there wasn't enough to make the game interesting. For boys, we found no single colour so ubiquitous, but the palette was still predictable—after a brief pastel phase in infancy, things moved pretty quickly into sports, army or 'character'-themed clothing, usually offered in institutional colours of mustard, khaki, and steel-blue.

Confronted with these marketing assumptions we got serious, especially about raising a girl. How would we make space for her to have both vulnerability and competence? We talked about the peer pressure to be girly, and how, in a family with two non-femme parents, she might feel pressure to be androgynous or butch. How might we support a femme girl without the baloney that comes with beauty culture?

I ordered some bright sleepers in bold colours from an online boutique. I found that with financial means, there were options for whimsical or unisex clothing. Working class boy clothing seemed to reinforce a very stereotypical picture of physical butch masculinity, but a more nuanced masculinity appeared to be available to young men in families of means. The clothes showed more diversity in fabric, print, and tailoring. I was working my first professional job out of university, and we had the financial privilege to make whimsical clothing choices, but I had grown up in poverty. The contrast was very striking. Even still, we didn't really talk about parenting a boy.

When we came home, in the exhausted blur the post-partum period, we promised we'd figure it out. We said we'd "try to raise one of the good guys." But what did that mean, and how would it inform our parenting?

* * *

Growing up, I didn't understand gender. What a strange, inflexible system for sorting people! It was rife with contradictions, bad at matching people to their greatest passion and skill. I knew from stories and schoolyard warnings that it was dangerous to step too far outside your gender's role. The world responded with mockery, dismissal, or even violence. Yet, within each gender role, the rules and attributes were shifting and inconsistent.

I understood the civil justice implications of biological sex and sexual orientation. My activist parents made it clear that civil rights were only recently being gained for women and people of colour, and their politics informed my play. I knew playing knights in the forest with my male friends was 'tomboyish,' which was an okay word, but when they played with dolls with me they weren't 'sissy,' because that was a bad and ignorant word.

In high school I enjoyed the free androgyny of New Wave, Glam, and Goth. I had no problem with either butch or femme as expressions and didn't see them as necessary expressions for men and women because their association to a sexual binary seemed like a cultural hangover. I knew that the construction worker couldn't show up in eyeliner without being called a "fag," but I had confidence that the old ideas were going fallow and in 20 years' time we'd be past them, just like we were past poodle skirts and hair grease. Annie Lennox and David Bowie were leading the way.

Historically, this was an innocent viewpoint, but it made sense with the information I had. After all, gender was a contradictory bunch of category definitions. When commenting that porn seemed predominantly made for male consumption, I was told that men were simply more 'visual,' and yet the joke was also made that men were boors when it came to aesthetics, uninterested in clothing choice and wall colour. And how were women supposed to be hysterical, silly, or careless creatures, and also the emotional centre of families? I could see from the men and women around me that caring for a family took patience, thought, empathy, and care. Similarly, the idea of a woman behind every great man created tension. If we were disadvantaged emotionally and intellectually, shouldn't we be the tantrum throwing rock stars, with stable, steadfast men in support?

Then there were stereotypes challenged by the people in my life. Women were less handy, but my mother taught me to change washers and find the studs in walls. I loved working on the engine of our old Honda Civic with my stepfather, and no one blinked an eye when I replaced a clutch cable. And what of men unable to speak their feelings? I knew male poets and writers and psychologists who earned their livings with thoughts and words about feelings.

Often I found the contradictions hilarious, an eccentric delusion, a game of pretend that some adults were insistent on playing even as it hurt them. Then puberty made it all serious. Sexual rules were contradictory and clearly not built for me. I liked orgasms, thought about sex, wasn't promiscuous, and didn't like dressing femme. Did that make me a slut, male, frigid, or a dyke? I had no clue, but just knew I hated being treated 'like a girl,' complimented, cajoled, and treated like the sexual prize at the end of a slick set of words.

As I transitioned into the world of university and of work, I saw how butch and femme were linked tightly to money. They weren't a joke; they were business. Femme stuff was masculine when done professionally: women sewed but men were surgeons. Women cooked but men were chefs. High femme costuming wasn't my thing, and it was also clearly expensive and hard to maintain in menial jobs: painted nails chip on working hands, and changing beds in high heels is hard on the back. A co-worker once suggested that I take on the vacuuming because "women are just better at the detail stuff," and I responded by laughing. Clearly men should be barred from all sorts of detail work if this were true, like neurosurgery, accounting, artistry, design, engineering, and cabinetmaking! The observation was not well received. Suddenly I was an activist, and I hadn't meant to be.

My reaction to this insistence that my biological sex was so important to my role in the world was rather odd; I didn't like being an inadvertent activist. Rather than rebelling, I started wondering. Was my mockery of these systems wrong? I began to think my idea that gender was a quickly passing fad was a tad naïve, and so I reconsidered the idea that the butch and femme were cultural. Maybe there was something inbuilt behind this relentless juggernaut of gender, genes that expressed themselves by admiring both throw pillows and men's penises. Perhaps I was just a late bloomer and my biological sex was going to come along and lay out my preferences and abilities for me, one gendered role at a time.

* * *

My eldest son was just ten months old. We were in a clothing store, wandering and looking at things, taking refuge from the rain and getting out of the house. We were touching different fabrics to see what they were like. "Smooth," I said. "Rough." "Blue."

It was just before Halloween, and in one area of the store there was a collection of dramatic clothing. A bunch of boas draped over a stand, dragging their feather-tips on the floor like a huge weeping willow. I ran my fingers through them and my son giggled as they moved. He stroked them and found they were tickly. A red boa with glitter caught his attention; he laughed himself silly, a delightful open laugh, as I shook it. The feathers bounced and danced with the movement.

"Lovely little girl," someone said, behind me. I turned and found an older woman beaming at us. I was happy to talk to anyone using full sentences, and there was nothing better than sharing the joy of babies with anyone who wanted to listen. The woman had grandkids of her own, and we talked about their ages and how quickly they grew. But then I used the pronoun, "he."

"Oh, goodness, he's a boy? Aren't you worried, you know, that he'll…" She made a gesture with her hand: A limp sort of wave.

I winced, and said it was fine with me if he was. Our social temperature dropped and we took our leave. Walking home, with the baby asleep in the stroller, I breathed through a tight knot inside me; anger, yes, and also a problem I couldn't quite define. The homophobia was offensive, but there was something else at issue. There is a particular sexuality to the feather boa that made stark the problem between gender roles and presumed sexuality. After all, boas are often used flirtatiously on men: wearing them may be femme, but enjoying them is not exclusively female, otherwise they would only be a prop for gay women. Being denied the sensual femme, having it linked only to women, struck me as a hole I didn't want to dig in my boy's psyche.

Added to this, I didn't like the idea that wearing or enjoying femme things should be read as an invitation to be the object of male sexual gaze. Only in a universe where dressing femme invites active and intrusive male sexual attention do you have to protect a child from developing an attachment to feather boas.

I didn't want to see my son directed into life by the tyranny of small looks and open questions and I didn't want him growing up thinking of femme as alien and apart. I didn't want him to be told he couldn't prefer the soft, the cute, the pretty, or the fabulous because he is male. It may be a small seeming restriction, but I think it is more—it is a cultural lock on the door to domesticity, and it places both sex and home in the hands of women.

Children learn by playing. If femme is segregated to girls, then women will develop comfort with femme as a result of their play as girls that boys do not. I saw this in my relationship: when we first came home with the baby, both my partner and I felt overwhelmed and joked that we couldn't believe they'd let such rank amateurs take the baby home. Yet I recovered from this more quickly, buoyed by social expectation and a lifetime of playing at caretaking. In comparison, my partner felt weighted down with the stereotype of man as blundering parent, and the world reflected this to him when he went out with our child: he came home deflated as he was often congratulated for simple things like remembering the diaper bag. He was presented with an expectation of inability, of 'babysitting' his son, of being amazing for 'helping' at home. I seemed the 'natural' intermediary, the priestess of child interpretation; it was expected that I could decipher what a particular cry meant, and 'know' the right ritual of jiggling and rocking in response. The idea that I should step in and get the baby to bed, step in and tell my partner what to do, was tempting to both of us. At times it seemed the easy solution, since I was the one at home during the day. My partner and son figured it out, in time. I didn't need to stand between as interpreter and mystic. As my partner and son figured out their own communication, they found different solutions, different rituals, than mine.

In a similar way, if the sensual trappings around sexuality are seen as femme, women can be required as an intermediary to sexual expression. From early play, girls are given access to the tools of sexual theatre: some women are able to develop and use these tools of sexual promise to great effect. As a younger woman I heard a number of young men suggest there was a sexual power imbalance in women's favor; that women got to be choosy, and demand economic and romantic behaviours from men that they could not demand from us.

The equation frustrated me. I didn't want my power to come through sex work; it seemed to me clear that the 'sexual power' offered was limited to a small set of women (of particular age, class, size, orientation, race, and ability) and so was of limited and frangible utility. It also seemed clear that the "sexual power" on offer didn't extend to my physical safety, or even to my own pleasure and orgasm. Complex relationships needed to be figured out in order for either of us to be fulfilled. Where was the imbalance?

As a parent of a young boy, this became a different question. I didn't want my own privileged kids to grow up feeling powerless with women and assuming that women's greatest power was in sexual trade. I wished my kids to see their sexual relationships as respectful and fun. It seemed obvious to me that desire can make people feel powerless to it, but how was it that men of my youth saw women as wildly different in this regard?

I believe that when the sensual objects in sexual theatre are branded femme, and when a boy is routinely discouraged from indulging in softness and sensuality until he is old enough to embrace a woman, some aspect of his sensual, sexual self has been given to women to hold as an intermediary. Again, 'woman' functions as a priestess, a pass key to communication, only this time with a foundational aspect of self. When someone suggests boys should repress such sensual explorations because they're afraid of homosexuality, they're compounding the tale: there is nothing inherently femme about men being attracted to other men. Yet in the fear, there's the assumption that at least one gay man must become a false woman, stealing the priestesses' robes, to provide access to the temple.

And so I became a guard on the border of my son's expression of self. I was going to hold space for as long as I could and offer as many options as possible. Truthfully, gender is more of a rising floodwater than something I could fight, but I sandbagged as fast and as hard as I could, to try to keep the seeping judgement from curling around his heart.

Some of this space-keeping meant ensuring my children weren't an experiment or a mockery, that they not be in the line of fire of people with limp wristed insinuations. I wasn't perfect at keeping my own experience of gender from affecting my son's choices: when he wondered why he couldn't have a purple satin skirt covered in rhinestones like his best friend did, I pressed a purple satin cape into his hands and muttered an excuse about being a mom who didn't want to take care of such fancy clothes. I just didn't want to subject him to scrutiny. I didn't want to break his trust that I keep him safe by saying it was fine and sending him out to possible mockery or disdain.

We teach our children in stages; we let them use butter knifes before bread knifes, teaching them at every step how to be safe and confident before they take on greater risk and responsibility. But I have my own confidence levels and ability levels, too: I could handle dolls and dress-ups in a way that made me confident that he could too. A purple satin skirt seemed too much of a challenge for him, too edged for a child of his age; truthfully it is too edged for me. I would be self-conscious, and my smart, sensitive child would likely notice.

* * *

For the first many years of my children's lives we lived in the West End of Vancouver, a queer friendly neighbourhood.

The first visible constant of gendered messaging, ubiquitous and clear, is women as aesthetic object; slender, young, mostly white, cosmetic wearing women are a pervasive presence on magazine covers, billboards, and advertisements. There was simply no way for me to fight that onslaught, but living in a queer neighbourhood meant there were also aesthetic images of sexy men and real-world examples of male glamour. At home, my sister made sure our dress-up boxes were stuffed with all sorts of costumes, for cowboys and fire fighters, nurses and fairies. We stayed away from Disney, and even from Pixar for the first few years, avoiding messages where the bands of heroes are male and the women are singular quirky love interests.

It was hard and highly detailed work to try to create a non-binary environment. So much of our world is gendered in bizarre ways. (Yogurt is a girl food! Beer is a boy drink!) In childhood the lesson isn't subtle. Pink and blue aggressively segregate in toy stores. There are further rules: if it's a butterfly, a ladybug, or a dragonfly, then it's for girls. If it's spiders, caterpillars, or beetles, it's for boys. It was a point of pride for us that we made it to potty training and pull ups and my son sometimes chose the pink pull-ups with butterflies, and sometimes the blue ones with motorcycle ATVs. Running interference without making a big deal of it was hard work, and required my best acting besides: it was important to me that I stayed, where possible, neutral on what small choices my kids were making. I didn't want to push femme, just leave it an open option.

When I am told by people that gender must be inherent because they've seen it in young kids, I want to fall down laughing. I failed to stop the onslaught, and I was working hard. Creating a genderless universe in our culture is as theoretical as creating a frictionless one. But I did lower the atmospheric pressure for my first son until kindergarten, when we learned that Hello Kitty socks were over the line of what was acceptable.

* * *

The omnipresence of gender roles bewildered me: why had they not faded since my childhood like poodle skirts and hair grease? However, being pregnant and parenting the first two years of my son's life revealed one major trick of gender; as an unwieldy pregnant woman and then a new mom with a small, dependent life nestled around me breastfeeding, I felt more vulnerable and in need of care than I had done since I was a child. My great-grandmothers all had many babies, as many as twelve, and had nursed each for more than a year. I imagined spending two decades of a short life in that state of vulnerability, and imagined all the work necessary for helping those children grow. Suddenly, the gender roles made more sense; I could see their outlines in my sudden, crashing lifestyle change.

I was necessary to this infant in a way that restricted my movement and twinned me to a small and milky routine. I could see why outside things might become men's roles: tucked all day into home, I could see all the home things that needed doing in a way my partner couldn't. I could see how a basket of sewing was easier to make safe with a toddler around than sharp edged tools and splintery wood. My husband and I had been clear that whoever worked as the primary caregiver was neither housekeeper nor cook, but when I wasn't working in the paid labour force (and after the newborn period) it ended up fitting into my days. Many of the household chores fell comfortably, but not exclusively, to me.

I found it bizarre that the experience *wasn't* hell. I loved exploring the world with my son, the serious scowl of concentration on his face as he thought. I loved holding his chubby body to mine and feeling him go boneless while he relaxed into sleep. I even loved domestic organization, the system building of home, making our world flow more easily and cheaply and healthfully. As he grew, I had to be creative to both facilitate my son and to socialize him to express himself without hurting others. I was teaching him to be responsible to his community: this was philosophical work that re-engaged me to the world. It was hugely challenging work, but hugely rewarding, too.

I started talking about this work with other primary caregivers, one of whom was my father-in-law, homeschooling his eight-year-old son. He had been the breadwinner for years with his oldest children, sometimes taking on more than one job and seeing his family rarely. When a baby came as a surprise into his middle age, he and my mother-in-law decided to try a different path, and he took to primary caregiving like a duck to water. He, as I, was surprised by both the challenge and the joy he was finding in the role.

Society is set up in a way that infers that nurturing and domestic roles are torture to any but the dim-witted. With many people pointing to duty and God as reasons for traditional roles, and penalties for women outside the home, it doesn't sound like it's going to be a satisfying life. There is an implication in the coercion that denies women financial and political rights that no one would choose a woman's lot: forced marriage, lack of property and voting rights, lack of equal pay or the right to drive, these patriarchal rules advertise that domesticity is something that can only be done by a slave class. Feminists have to work so hard to win the most basic of rights.

So I was astounded to discover it could be fun; not just the childrearing, but the domesticity. The only prison is in lack of choice: with the door open so that I could choose, domestic life seemed great place to work awhile. I only wish the door was open a little wider, so that my partner also had the flexibility. And so my agnosticism about gender has returned. Some of the roles are understandable afterimages of a different time, but they clearly do not define all of us, or even most of us, over a lifetime.

* * *

I thought that living in a liberal, queer allied neighbourhood was going to make gender pressure far less relevant, but that was not the case. It kept arriving in ways I didn't expect. Sometimes it seemed I was watching a mutual hallucination in gender, even when evidence to the contrary was before us.

Christmas parties in our community room always featured boy toys and girl toys; it's hard to avoid them. One year my son traded his gift with a girl, exchanging his military set for a bright spinning LED toy. He stared into it, hypnotized, as the girl proceeded to strategize the military end to the party. A neighbour bemused me by remarking how brilliant boys were at their war games.

A few years later I attended a birthday party for my older son's closest friend, the girl who lived next door to us. The adults at the party were diverse: gay and straight, male and female, recent immigrants and Canadian born, working and stay at home parents. Our friend unwrapped her presents, and then left them so she could run about with the other kids at the party.

My younger son, just two-years old, stayed close to me eyeing the gifts. He really wanted to get to one of the two dolls. I had to stop him from opening the package, explaining it was our friend's present, but I could see the attraction. The doll had a bottle and the ability to close her eyes, which his didn't. I don't know whether it was prompted by my male child's interest in the presents, or whether it was just the bounty in front of us, but one of the moms started talking about how interesting it was that girls loved sparkles and baby dolls, even in this new age of equal rights and feminist possibility. Other parents nodded and agreed, while I held my son back from stealing gifts and bit my tongue.

There was no evidence of the girls loving sparkles and baby dolls at the party. I knew the child in question pretty well: she and my eldest had come through a baby-doll phase while I was pregnant, and neither was terribly interested anymore. In front of me was evidence of people buying generic girl presents, not anything inherent to the birthday girl, who was appropriately thankful but not thrilled. All of these presents multiplied over all the birthday parties that these kids had attended and were little lessons in gender that became a high pressure system in their social organizing: I'm thinking about this all the time and walk carefully on that border, myself, picking neutral art or science presents for kids I don't know well. Buying a 'cross-gender' toy that might create teasing for being unusual would wound the kid who wanted it most. Plus, it's not just teasing of kids, but the benign-seeming discussion of adults: my littlest was with us hearing parents discuss girls and dolls. He knew he was a boy, and his ears were open. He was being told something about the way the world worked.

Later, I brought this up, and everyone agreed we should be careful not to bully the young ones who have 'different' preferences. We should protect, defend, and stand up for our unusual children, who may be gay or trans. Compliments to my children were made. Of course this is true but is was not what I was saying: I'm parenting children I hope are empathetic, loving, nurturing people, even if they're straight, cis-gendered, and male. We don't need to abandon our non-queer boy children to expectations devoid of gentleness and nurturing, or our non-queer girl children to expectations devoid of kick-ass risk taking. We don't *need* to expect a limited maleness, a limited femaleness, and we *are* telling them who to be. We shouldn't only support those brave enough, self-aware enough, and attracted enough to the opposite-grouping that they push back at a young age.

My boys are very often praised as great kids and I agree that they are. They're normal kids, as prone to misbehaviour and random energy and temper tantrums as anyone, but they are also sensitive, empathetic young men. Some of this is inherent to who they are as people, but some of this is also in our rules. I heard "well, that's what boys are like" more than once in the liberal West End from people I know as powerful and thoughtful. When a completely unacceptable behaviour was unfolding, I found it most troubling: my boys do not get to hit each other, ignore other people's feelings, or bully other kids because they have penises. A penis is not a magic wand that makes responsibility disappear.

* * *

When my youngest was three, we moved out to Marpole—a much more conservative neighbourhood. Most of my neighbours are first or second generation immigrants from the Philippines or China. We are a mix of classes—working class renters, and upper class owners.

In this more conservative neighbourhood, my boys are sometimes obvious gender eccentrics. My youngest likes to put colourful paint on his nails in stripy patterns, and both wear bead bracelets they buy every summer on Hornby Island. The hairstyles here for boys tend to be very short: my eldest is currently sporting a pompadour and a rat tail, and my youngest a "Justin Bieber" haircut. They've received commentary on their choices, but not teasing.

The tone about gender is different. I don't know why—it could be that mockery happens in Tagalog or that I'm being scolded in gentle ways that fly over my head. Perhaps we're given room coming from a different cultural background, or perhaps that I'm a writer affords us artistic privilege.

Yet inherent conservatism means that gender jamming is being noticed more often. Bizarrely, that's way more comfortable for me than the feeling of mass delusion, of inability to see what was happening, or the "excuse" that I might have a gay or trans child. I feel like my children are actually being seen based on their behaviour, rather than their assumed behaviour, and it's localized to the moment. A conversation might run: "That's different, your boy wears nail polish," and I answer, "yes he does; he likes to make patterns in the paint" and we nod and move on. Remarks on my lovely, polite boys are common, and definitely in a gendered context: I have had parents of girls apologize for their unladylike female children, when my kids take a following role in a game. I tell them that I think their girls are wonderful, and that my kids are clearly having fun.

The male friends of my boys sometimes do schoolyard gender policing, and we talk about it when the kids come home. Both of my kids have areas they don't want to invite teasing, and confident areas where what they do is their own business and they stand up for themselves. Working culture through with friends strikes me as a very good use of school time, as long as bullying doesn't come into play.

My husband and I may have started out our parenting experience hoping to raise "one of the good ones," but we are also trying to raise people who can find a place for themselves in society where they can contribute and be happy. This means outfitting them with the tools to choose what is right for them and the critical faculties to think about and defend their choices. That work is beginning for them in the schoolyard, as it did for me when I was young.

How do any of us handle opposition, ridicule, or a restrictive cultural expectation? I don't think there's a single human answer to these questions. Our answers come from living our lives, stumbling, and righting ourselves again. Our answers come from our vision of what's possible and our commitment to try. We are not islands in a cultural sea, but rather people in relationships and the play-ground is practice in negotiating, in standing firm, in giving way.

The rule in our house is that we don't exclude people for things they cannot change. We might stay away from people who are behaving in a cruel way, and we tend to hang out with people who have similar interests, but we don't snub or shun people because of who they are. Like all rules of our home, this one has needed testing on the schoolyard: it didn't make much sense to my youngest until he found friends excluded from a "club" of friends because they were girls. At first, he went along with the idea, and did not tell us. Eventually it got to him: he created his own club, gave it an even cooler secret handshake, and felt much better when all his friends could join. This exclusion and inclusion play went on over the course of a month, and I listened and challenged some of the ideas that he was bringing home, but he had to test the boundaries we'd given him before making them his own.

So has my attempt to raise children with choice of self-expression made a difference to their lives?

I think it has. At eleven and seven, I can't sandbag the encroach-ment of gender for them and I don't try; instead we talk about it as it comes up. Now that they are making their own way, I try to listen and question, more than suggest. I've watched the boys make small compromises: like when my youngest decided pink is a challenging favorite colour, but red is okay, or when my eldest stopped sketching ladybugs and started sketching scarab bee-tles because they were more butch. I make sure I reaffirm that I think these categories are cultural, not biological. As long as they know I think it's arbitrary, I don't criticize their choices. For my boys, there have been months where fitting in matters more than standing ground for their own preferences, and then some small circumstance will come up and the boys will suddenly question and resist their gender socialization, claiming "girly" things for their own.

My younger son has been at times fairly skeptical of our insis-tence that there are no 'girl' or 'boy' toys, even though some of his favourite toys, like his dollhouse, would be gendered to most. In Grade One, with the gentle manner of someone softening the blow of bad news, he explained that we've got it wrong, that boys and girls have different interests because they're boys and girls.

I validated that he's seeing real segregation: denying the existence of this won't help him deal with it. It's a simple conversation after that: noting only that there's a big difference between 'most' and 'all.' Every segregated interest he's mentioned, he's also been able to find a counter example of someone of the opposite sex who likes that toy or activity. It was helpful for him to hear that I liked playing Dungeons & Dragons as a kid, or that his uncle liked to knit. In these conversations he's remembered times when he's gotten the idea he shouldn't spend too much time with a "girl" thing, and we explore what that feels like. The embarrassment is the socialization. He often remembers when a friend found out he has a Fidget Friend, a toy marketed to girls, and the feeling he had to give it up or deny interest in order to get along.

My elder son is confronting ideas of masculinity at a middle school level, trying to figure out who he is and how he fits in with peers. These days, discussions are more nuanced than 'girl' toys and 'boy' toys. He is instead dealing with the idea of social hierarchy, acceptance in society, and what sort of identity is important to embrace. This movement towards understanding himself in his own peer context, rather than in the communities we've created as a family, means that he's searching for his own path through. As puberty starts making itself known in his class and peer group, sexual difference is going to get increasingly powerful—that would be ridiculous to deny! Our talk has shifted to matters of orientation, dating, and relationships.

The best I can do is help equip these children to make their way through life and culture with respect for themselves and others. In talking and thinking about these issues, I see confidence, respect, and a base rejection of too-small labels. It gives me hope that indeed, they have a chance at being 'good guys'—open, communicative, and respectful of themselves and those around them.

11.
I Wish I Knew How to
Make Cabbage Rolls

An Explanation of Why The Future
of Ethnicity Relies Upon Gender Fluidity

SARAH SAHAGIAN

I WAS BORN WITH MORE THAN ONE ethnic background. It was a fact about myself that was so obvious I couldn't hide it even if I had wanted to. My name, Sarah Emily Laidlaw Sahagian, metaphorically tattooed two basic facts onto my identity: that my parents had decided I was a girl by choosing traditionally feminine given names, and that I possessed Anglo-Saxon and Armenian ancestry judging by my surnames. Just because I was born with ancestors from more than one ethnicity, however, does not mean that the manner in which I was raised reflected this in a meaningful way. When you are predominately raised by a stay-at-home mom in Toronto who knows nothing about Armenian people besides the fact that she became related to some by marriage when she was 26, it is all too easy to grow up more WASP than a character on *Downton Abbey*.

As I detailed in my 2012 journal article, "What's in a Last Name? Patriarchy, Interethnicity and Maternal Training," I grew up immersed in elements of WASP culture like earl gray tea, scones and BBC historical miniseries, but my last name and swarthy looks made it difficult for WASP people to see me as one of them. They seemed to think I was some sort of pretender despite the fact that my mother had exposed me to pretty much every element of her heritage that her own mother had taught her to embrace. When it came to hanging out with Armenians, however, I actually was a pretender. I knew so little of what it meant to be Armenian that my last name felt like a fraud, a false promise to the world. A name that made other Armenian people excited to meet me, shrieking in enthusiastic tones, speaking fast and foreign words, as I was forced to reply in an awkward and ashamed voice, "I'm sorry, but I don't actually know how to speak the language. I never learned." Invariably, I would then meet with puzzled expressions, and, by way of explanation, I would invariably feel compelled to reply, "My mother isn't Armenian at all."

These feelings of inadequacy can be unpleasant to recall. After all, I was a girl who supposedly had multiple ethnicities but was not fully accepted anywhere. This feeling of rejection, however, proved to be quite productive for me. As I have grown as a person and become an academic who studies motherhood and ethnic hybridity, it is this personal feeling of ethnic inadequacy that has inspired and driven me. What I will contend in this paper is that children with inter-ethnic backgrounds may miss out on some of their cultural history in the absence of gender fluid parenting—both in childhood and for the rest of their lives. It is not easy to teach oneself one's family history, the mother tongue of one's ancestors, how to cook traditional foods or celebrate traditional holidays. In a world wedded to binary gender norms that construct the task of cultural training as work that ought to be done by women as mothers, the idea of an inter-ethnic child who is meaningfully acquainted and connected with all of her ethnic communities might sound like a fantasy. But fantasies are a powerful starting point for reinventing our reality. The point of this piece is to imagine new ways of conceiving inter-ethnicity. It is time to imagine a new world, one where the preservation of ethnicity does not depend on the institutions of heterosexuality and endogamy as it has in the past. And in order to imagine that world where ethnicity can survive inter-ethnic reproduction, it is important to embrace gender fluid parenting. After all, in a world where gender is more fluid, there is a hope that ethnicity can be so as well.

While I am about to detail how I think a more gender fluid upbringing could have helped me develop a more robust sense of my own ethnic identity, I am under no illusions that being raised this way would not have had its own set of obstacles. Growing up as a gender fluid child can be tricky too. As May Friedman illustrates in her chapter of this volume, raising one's children to embrace a more fluid sense of gender identity is not without its complications.

I understand the risks and realities of the situation. I know that not everyone who is part of an endangered ethnic community will necessarily think that gender fluidity is a good idea. Having said that, I would like to make my own case for why ethnicity matters, and for why our ethnic identities might be more robust and healthier if we were raised in a more gender fluid world.

Of course, one might ask, what is ethnicity, anyway? It seems such a broad concept, and frankly, it can be. Anthony Smith argues, "The 'core' of ethnicity ... resides in the quartet of 'myths, memories, values and symbols' and in the characteristics of styles and genres of certain historical configurations of populations" (15). Smith also contends that ethnic groups "always possess ties to a particular locus or territory, which they call their 'own'" (28). Finding a piece of land and developing a community with its own unique culture seems like something any one of us could do if we wanted. Indeed, if we were to stop the definition here, ethnicity as a concept would seem fairly inclusive. Ethnicity, however, does not simply require individual people who have chosen to commit to a certain territory and community; conceptions of heredity also play a central role in conceptions of ethnicity. Smith writes, "So long as a community can reproduce its members sufficiently from generation to generation, demographic continuity will ensure ethnic survival..." (96).

While there are times when the fact of my inter-ethnicity has seemed too daunting for me to come to terms with, I must admit to myself that I crave and desire parts of my ethnic identity in the visceral way one wants a lover. I have a yen for mulled wine at Christmas, but I also wish I knew how to make authentic Armenian pilaf for Easter. And yet, despite my desire, as a child of inter-ethnic background, *how can I have all of my ethnicities?* If merely wanting them were enough, my ethnicities could be mine in an uncomplicated way, but wanting ethnicity is never enough. Just like with a lover, in order to have the ethnicity you crave, that ethnicity has to *want you back*.

Ethnicity can be a gift that we give our children, but it is a gift we may not be able to give future generations unless we work consciously to make sure the way we construct and pass it down is allowed to evolve. Ethnicity does not have to be a fragile and breakable thing, the property of a body of people whose community weakens every time someone does not reproduce or has children with someone from another ethnic group. I do believe that the languages, ancient myths, traditions, holidays, songs and idioms associated with different ethnicities can show us unique ways of seeing. It is time to harness the elastic potential of ethnicity. As Rogers Brubaker argues, ethnicities are not so much "things *in* the world, but perspectives *on* the world" (17).

In theory, I do not favour my mother's ancestors over my father's, and yet, hers is disproportionately the ethnic perspective I grew up cultivating. Of course, it is in no way my mother's fault she was a stay-at-home mother whose husband worked 12-hour days. Nor is it her fault that she knew how to cook the same delicious Sunday roast beef dinner her grandmother used to make but had never heard of manti. It is also perfectly understandable that she grew up being taught about Camelot and the Loch Ness Monster but knew little of the Ancient Byzantine Empire. And yet, the fact that I love the family history my mother was able to impart to me does not make up for the great sorrow I feel over the fact that I do not know how to make dolma, an Armenian cabbage roll dish.

Dolma is one of my father's favourite things to eat. His grandmother made it for him when he was a child. She taught the younger women in the family how to make this dietary staple, but because he was a boy, it never occurred to my great-grandmother to teach my dad. Now that the matriarchs of my father's family have passed away, neither he nor I will ever get to taste that particular recipe again. There it is, a family ethnic tradition disappeared because of binary gender norms.

As Thomas Hylland Eriksen tells us, no society that anthropologists have ever studied operates freely of the concept of gender predicated on the binary assumption that men and women "need each other" to perform "complementary" roles (155). As I see it, the separation of men and women's work in any given culture is the key flaw in the organization of any given ethnocultural community. The greatest obstacle to preserving the different ways of seeing given to us by ethnicity is this extremely gendered way in which culture is transmitted to children. Nira Yuval Davis and Patrizia Albanese both argue in their work that women are the ones who come to perpetuate organizational collectivities such as ethnicities and nation-states. Yuval Davis writes, "As we have seen, women play crucial roles in biological, cultural and political reproduction of national and other collectivities" (630). She argues that women become a form of "'border guards'" (627). As such, women are the transmitters of group customs to future generations who "can signify ethnic and cultural boundaries" (627).

Of course, this quest for ethnic preservation women are tasked with is not only cultural, but involves maintaining the purity of the ethnic bloodline, as well. Albanese concludes: "The nation's future is believed to hinge upon the chastity of 'its' women—jealously guarded or protected from the ravaging hands of the 'Other'..." (830). If women were not the only ones tasked with cultural training, however, the patriarchal control of women's bodies that has historically been harnessed to preserve ethnocultural communities would become obsolete. Ethnic boundaries as they are currently constructed depend upon the gender binary, but I contend the true potential of ethnicity in the twenty first century can be unlocked with gender fluidity.

As an adult, I thought perhaps I could use my agency to overcome the limitations of my inter-ethnicity imposed on me by the intersection of ethnicity and the gender binary. After having spent a year living in London, UK, I realized that I had no problem making the perfect cup of English breakfast tea, watching BBC historical dramas and eating Yorkshire pudding for months on end. These were all elements of WASP culture my stay-at-home mother had familiarized me with on a daily basis from birth. Even though WASP people themselves did not always accept me as one of them because of my inter-ethnicity, I was at least culturally literate in Anglo-Saxon traditions. While I reveled in my love of bagpipes and scones during the immersion in British culture that my year abroad afforded me, this is also precisely the time when the feeling of being ethnically lopsided became too much for me to bear. I moved back to Canada with two goals: the first was to earn my Ph.D. in Gender Studies at York University, and the second was to live out my inter-ethnicity in my daily life.

Unfortunately, my attempts to become an Armenian adult without ever having been an Armenian child were less successful than

I had hoped they would be. I tried to teach myself Armenian at the age of twenty-three, but it is an exceedingly difficult language for a native English-speaker to grasp. The new alphabet proved impossible to me and no matter how hard I worked at it, my accent never really improved. Eventually I gave up altogether when some people I knew argued that when it came to learning Armenian it was simply "too late for me." I do not know if this was in fact true, but when I looked around, comparing myself to those who had been taught this language from their infancy, it felt like there was no way to catch up, to know the nuances and beauty of this language as meaningfully as they did. If I would always be behind everyone in the diasporic Armenian community, why should I devote so much of my time to learning this new tongue? Is it not the purpose of learning a language to converse with others who speak it? Why should I expect them to dumb down their conversations to indulge me! Whether it was rational to think so or not, part of me simply felt too embarrassed to continue my studies. Learning Armenian was a test I began to feel my upbringing had set me up to fail.

I thought if I could not speak Armenian, then maybe I could at least become what I ate. I trolled the Internet for new Armenian recipes, but having never tried many of the more complicated dishes before, I had no reference point for whether or not I was even making them properly. I also tried attending events at Armenian cultural centers from historical lectures to film festivals, but I found that most of the people there had spent their lives attending Armenian private schools and going to traditional dances at the holidays. While I was very grateful for the friends I did make there, most of the people I connected with were in fact only part Armenian, like me. We bonded over our hybridity. Some of our parents had been more successful than others in teaching us to embrace and perform our multiple ethnicities, but all of us expressed some degree of awkwardness surrounding navigating our ethnic identities. In some ways, it was less our Armenianness and more our lack of it that united us.

Ultimately, in my own experience I found it very challenging to make up for lost time and opt into joining an ethnic community as an adult. The tasks and customs of *being* an ethnicity must be performed, and in order for one to engage in such a performance, one must know how, which requires having been *taught* how, ideally from birth. The socially constructed norm that women as mothers are the ones who perform cultural training is damaging, of course, as is the gender-specific way in which we raise our children. Teaching only little girls ethnic cooking and handicrafts with the expectation that little girls will pass on these ethnic traditions to their own children one day only works in a non-existent world where inter-ethnic unions never occur and where compulsory heterosexuality characterizes all family formations.

Eriksen has posited that in an era where inter-ethnic marriages and reproduction have become so common, ethnicity as a concept might go extinct. Gender fluid parenting, however, is one strategy for reforming and salvaging ethnicity. What do I mean by gender fluid parenting as a means of preserving ethnicity? For me, gender fluid parenting is two-pronged. First, I contend it requires that the work of cultural training and primary care-giving no longer be reserved for women in ethnocultural groups. People of all genders must be allowed and encouraged to participate in the cultural training of their children so that if a child has more than one ethnicity, that child will also have a better opportunity to have been culturally trained and immersed in all of his/her/zer various backgrounds. Secondly, we require a world where gender fluid cultural training is the norm. We require a world where all children are equipped with the necessary skills and knowledge to be culture bearers themselves; a world where all children are raised to feel comfortable with their sexual preferences, whatever those may be, but are also raised with the expectation they will one day grow up to participate in the cultural training of their own children, should they choose to have any.

Gender fluid parenting protects ethnic traditions by sharing them with a broader range of people. As Andrea O'Reilly sees it, empowered mothers stand against "the gender roles that straight-jacket our children and the harm of sexism, racism, classism and heterosexism more generally" (50). In fact, she feels patriarchy resists empowered mothering "because it understands its real power to bring about a true and enduring cultural revolution" (50). I see part of this cultural revolution of empowered mothering, one that includes gender fluid parenting, as creating the possibility of preserving ethnicity by reforming it into something that does not require mothers to be wedded to the institution of heterosexual endogamy.

I have come to see quite clearly how the fight to save ethnic identity is linked to the fight for a more gender fluid world. As someone who has spent a great deal of her life in the gender studies academy, I am fortunate enough to have been immersed in queer theory. I know that the heteronormative framework for sexual attraction is not the only one that exists. Just as there are people who identify as queer or bisexual, who feel they can be truly and meaningfully attracted to people from more than one gender, I feel inter-ethnic people can truly want and be all of their ethnicities at once. There is no reason a young woman who is of Chinese and French ancestry cannot celebrate both Chinese New Year and Bastille Day with equal enthusiasm. There is no reason why said person should not be able to study the philosophy of both Foucault and Confucius, practice fencing as well as Zi Ran Men boxing, and enjoy eating dim sum for lunch with a chocolate éclair for dessert. There is no need for inter-ethnic reproduction to be taboo. The fear that children with parents who belong to different ethnocultural groups will not know how to perform all of their ethnicities becomes baseless in a world where women are no longer raised to be the primary cultural bearers for the world. Ethnic hybridity, which I see as the blending of multiple ethnic identities in one person, can happen as long as it is accompanied by a new form of gender hybridity that does not seek to transform our children into performers of radically different social roles in our ethnocultural communities based on whether we believe they have a penis or a vagina at birth.

Of course the gender fluid parenting of inter-ethnic children may raise subjects who are more in touch with their various ethnic backgrounds, but we must also increase the fluidity of ethnicity itself. The logic of the gender binary is very similar to the logic of the ethnic binary, which divides the world into the categories of "Self" and "Other." I have discussed how the rigid borders ethnic-ities create around themselves, classifying some as members and others as outsiders are just as problematic as the binary sex-gender system that encourages people to believe their genders equate to their genitals. I believe, however, that the more children we raise to be proficient in multiple ethnicities, the more different ethnocultural communities will see that inter-ethnicity does not necessarily equate to the destruction of a given ethnocultural community. This might lead to more than the end of ethnicity's investment in compulsory heterosexual endogamy. If we see the self and other can and often do exist simultaneously in the bodies of inter-ethnic subjects, perhaps we might one day see a reduction in xenophobia in general. It is time to pursue the gender fluid strategies of cultural training that will allow us to see inter-ethnic children as symbolic bridges uniting different histories, people and places.

Ethnicity is part of the world's intellectual history. It is the languages our ancestors spoke, their recipes, their legends, their songs, their sports, their books, their art, their architecture, their superstitions, and their sayings. It is, however, somewhat ironic that ethnic borders were once largely constructed and maintained through the existence of a rigid gender binary, but the salvation of ethnicity likely lies in the destruction of these very same rigid gender roles. Ethnicity as we know it is at a turning point. For those of us who feel there are aspects of our ethnic perspectives we would like to salvage, there is much that can be done, but this quest must start in the home. When we strive to raise our children in a more gender fluid way, saving ethnicity from its own demise just may be the proverbial pot of gold at the end of the metaphorical rainbows we chase.

WORKS CITED

Albanese, Patrizia. "Territorializing Motherhood: Motherhood and Reproductive Rights in Nationalist Sentiment and Practice." *Maternal Theory: Essential Readings.* Ed. Andrea O'Reilly. Bradford: Demeter Press, 2007. 828-839. Print.

Brubaker, Rogers. *Ethnicity Without Groups.* Cambridge, MA: Harvard University Press, 2004. Print.

Eriksen, Thomas Hylland. *Ethnicity and Nationalism.* London: Pluto Press, 2002. Print.

O'Reilly, Andrea. *Rocking the Cradle*. Toronto: Demeter Press, 2006. Print.

Pettman, Jan Jindy. *Worlding Women: A Feminist International Politics*. New York: Routledge, 1996. Print.

Sahagian, Sarah. "What's in a Last Name? Patriarchy, Interethnicity and Maternal Training." *Journal of the Motherhood Initiative* 2.1 (2012): 55-56. Print.

Smith, Anthony. *The Ethnic Origin of Nations*. Oxford: Basil Blackwell, 1986. Print.

Yuval Davis, Nira. "Gender and Nation." *Ethnic and Racial Studies* 16.4 (1993): 621-632. Print.

12.
The Parental Transition

A Study of Parents of Gender Variant Children

ELIZABETH RAHILLY

I N A POST ON *Accepting Dad* (2011), a blog dedicated to one man's meditations on raising his gender-nonconforming son, the author Bedford Hope writes, "The existing literature on transgender people, books like *True Selves*, spoke only of adults, and only of adults who had been viciously suppressed as children. The end result—misery. While *True Selves* showed us how not to raise our kids; there were no books to tell us what we should be doing" (n. pag.). This parent, representative of a burgeoning population of parents who are actively supporting their gender-nonconforming children, speaks to a relative dearth of literature and history on childhood gender variance, particularly in a vein that is non-clinical and averse to pathology. There is, of course, substantial clinical history on "Gender Identity Disorder" (GID) in children, but this is lodged within the realms of psychiatry and psychology, or "psychopathology," as represented in Richard Green's infamous book, *The Sissy Boy Syndrome and the Development of Homosexuality*, which chronicles his decades-long research with feminine young boys and was largely influential in the development of the GID diagnosis. Outside of the mental health professions, or of critical analyses of their orientations (see, for example, Karl Bryant's "In Defense of Gay Children?"), there is limited social or cultural insight into gender-nonconforming children and the families who raise them—whether it is families who accept and nurture such behaviour, or treat it as a problem needing to be fixed. Indeed, it is only within the last ten years that the prospect of identifying, and raising, a pre-adolescent child as categorically "gender variant" or "transgender" has surfaced on the cultural scene, as captured in Tey Meadow's innovative ethnography. A wave of mental health professionals who explicitly endorse supportive, accepting approaches to childhood gender nonconformity, versus more reparative interventions, reflects this. Dr. Diane Ehrensaft's recent publication, *Gender Born, Gender Made: Raising Healthy Gender-nonconforming Children*, is emblematic of this growing affirmative paradigm among practitioners, one that is particularly transgender-aware.

Of course, previous studies have demonstrated that childhood gender behaviour is never so cut and dry as the boy/girl binary, such as Barrie Thorne's *Gender Play*, in which she observed elementary school children "cross the 'gender divide'" quite frequently (111). In a related vein, there is research that reveals that some families consciously try to resist traditional gender norms, such as Barbara Risman and Kristen Myer's study of "egalitarian" parents who "deconstruct[ed] gender not only by encouraging their daughters and sons to develop free from stereotypes but also by modeling such behaviour in their own social roles" (229). More recently, Emily Kane ("Policing Gender Boundaries") has found that many parents do try to widen the range of possibilities for their children, such as buying toy kitchen sets for their sons, although this progressive range has its limits, especially when it comes to male children. Ultimately, most parents fall back into the "gender trap," which Kane (*The Gender Trap*) describes as the cultural compulsion to adhere to binary categories of masculine and feminine presentations for boy and girl children, respectively; few parents are willing to breach the binary for the sake of their children's well-being among their peers. Notwithstanding, in all of these studies, the case of an explicitly identified "gender variant" or "transgender" child, one who might meet the criteria for "GID," remains under the analytic radar. Even among the well-intentioned progressive parents, the children are presumably, implicitly cisgender[1] and gender-normative. What happens when "boys" are embraced as *girls*, "girls" are embraced as *boys*, or children are raised as something less binary altogether?

In recent years, gender-nonconforming children have gained visibility, both in the media and in popular discourse. Part of the increase in attention around these children is a growing population of parents who support them and who reject traditional psycho-therapeutic interventions, much like the "accepting dad" above. Society's limiting gender norms, they argue, should be the target of treatment, not the children. I conducted in-depth interviews with 24 such parents who identify their child as either "gender variant" (some degree of gender-nonconforming) or "transgender" (express themselves full-time as the "opposite" gender), representing sixteen children total.[2] These parents represent a new brand of "gender-neutral," or "gender-fluid," parenting, which pushes against gender norms in profound ways, including making explicitly *transgender* identities and transitions possible and viable at an unprecedentedly early point in the life course. Their experiences mark a process I term the *parental transition:* At first, they seek to curb their children's gender nonconformity, carefully negotiating the boundaries of the gender binary, a balancing act I refer to as "gender hedging." Over time, however, parents develop new beliefs that challenge mainstream ideology about gender, adopting a more spectrum-oriented perspective. Ultimately, parents transition into passionate advocates of a more inclusive and fluid gender ideology for all—at home, at school, and in society at large.

THE PARENTAL TRANSITION

When I first embarked on this research, I attended an annual conference for parents of gender-variant children. In several of the sessions, I was struck by a recurrent admission on the part of the parents in which they described feeling as if they were undergoing a "transition," much more unsettling than any kind of transition their transgender child was going through. As one parent described, her child was not transitioning; rather, *she* was transitioning, and trying to "catch up" to what her child has always known. After several years of interviewing and analysis, I have come to see this as an apt description for the range of experiences, emotions, processes and beliefs that these parents undergo and take on, and from which they emerge as advocates of a particularly trans-aware gender ideology.

The concept of "transitioning" is not unfamiliar to issues of "transgender." Along with the transitions that trans people experience personally, there is literature that concerns the ways in which these transitions affect immediate others. This often refers to romantic partners,[3] but also includes relationships with cisgender relatives, such as parents and other grown family members.[4] Because of the relatively "new" possibility of thinking about young children as "transgender," few works explore the "transitions" that gender-normative adults undergo in relation to their young gender-nonconforming children; only within the last few years has a handful of such narratives cropped up, such as Rachel Pepper's edited collection, *Transitions of the Heart: Stories of Love, Struggle and Acceptance by Mothers of Transgender and Gender Variant Children.*

Interestingly enough, themes relevant to these experiences have surfaced in literatures less familiar to the turf of transgender studies and more so to parents who are different from their children in some socially salient way or whose children differs from mainstream cultural norms, in particular white parents of Black or biracial children or able-bodied parents of children with disabilities. As these literatures attest, parents with these profiles develop a politicized consciousness around certain social categories and norms—in this instance, around race and (dis)ability, respectively—which they did not necessarily have before. As Melanie Panitch observed of the mothers of children with disabilities in her study, "They did not start out to change the world; they started out trying to secure better services for their children. They became 'accidental activists' when they reached a turning point … that expanded their consciousness beyond themselves … to include a wider web of associations with others" (6). Parents also adopt a variety of practices to instill pride in their child's or family's "difference" from their peers, as well as to educate their children about related societal prejudices and beliefs. France Winndance Twine writes extensively about this in terms of white parents' "racial literacy" with their biracial children in Britain, through which children learn a critical awareness about race, as well as develop pride in African diasporic culture and history (92).[5]

Parents' raised cultural and political awareness, as well as their institutional maneuverings on behalf of their children, are both themes that strongly parallel the kinds of radical transformations that cisgender parents of gender variant-identified children undergo. As such, the growing population of parents who embrace and accommodate their gender-nonconforming children presents an important and analytically promising intersection between transgender studies and and research on parenting and childhood socialization, especially in terms of "transitioning." It is around this concept that I have organized parents' stories.

GENDER HEDGING: NEGOTIATING THE GENDER BINARY

When recalling the early phases of their journeys, many of the parents I interviewed articulated practices I have come to term *"gender hedging,"* which refers to the compromises, strategies, and at times creative work that parents engage in to accommodate their gender-nonconforming child while not at the same time slipping too far into gender-transgressive territory. Almost all of the parents engaged in some form of this prior to encountering the greater affirmative community regarding childhood gender variance.[6] When engaging in gender hedging, parents draw various lines and boundaries to curtail their child's gender-atypical behaviours, engaging in a tricky negotiation of the gender binary. This might involve curbing the extent of the nonconformity (i.e. allowing a pink tee shirt instead of a dress) or limiting the degree to which gender variance goes public and gets noticed. In these hedging strategies, gender is less a natural given for the parents and more a daily negotiation in the accomplishment of their child's normativity—or what Kane might call "producing socially acceptable gender performances" ("Policing Gender Boundaries" 239). Ally[7] testified to the boundary work that this kind of hedging involves, or the "push-pull" along a masculine-feminine continuum, to keep one's child from seeming "too girly" (or "too boyish") in the eyes of others:

> [W]e were like, where are we gonna draw the line on things, what can he wear, where, with which people ... so we were setting boundary lines and then moving 'em back, and then panicking and moving 'em forward again, and so it was a push-pull, push-pull.... I think what we were

174

wondering about was, where was that line where it would quote "bother" people.

Beth, who was in many ways an exemplar of these kinds of practices, described hedging as "a daily tightrope act walk … [a] very difficult tightrope act," and a "fine line that we walk." Beth shared with me a variety of activities and interests that she and her husband have tried to regulate, often to her unease. For example, their son Tim (gender-variant male, five years old)[8] really wanted a Disney princess bike, but she and her husband were uncomfortable with him riding it around the neighborhood. As a "compromise," Beth suggested to Tim a plain, solid-colour bike, which she could outfit with a detachable Barbie basket. Beth fashioned similar compromises regarding dressy shoes for Tim. Instead of formal girls' shoes, she bought him pink sandals with Disney princesses on them, which he is allowed to wear "if he goes over to a girl-friend's for a play date, but he can't wear them to [summer] camp, he can't wear them normally." Like the bike, the shoes index the kind of strategic work that Beth engages in to accommodate her child's more feminine preferences without straying too far outside gender-normative constraints. These examples highlight the types of boundaries parents hedge around, including the degree of "girli-ness" and the degree it goes public. Similarly, Theresa recalled her efforts to "hold back the tide" of her daughter's (transgender girl, ten years old) femininity, such as choosing "aqua" over "pink":

> [S]o I started thrift shopping for things that were not super girly but in the girls' department … sort of more neutral … I was really trying to enforce a balance, I was trying not to go all the way into girly-girly land … I tried to hold back the tide.

While many parents exhibited this kind of hedging in the early phases of their journeys, I was intrigued to learn that several parents still believe in the need for some modification in certain public contexts, even now that they have embraced their child's gender-variant or cross-gender expression. Josie was one propo-nent of this:

> I do feel like ... he needs to be cognizant of his environment
> ... [while] I want to encourage him to express himself freely
> ... I also feel like, you know, he needs to understand that
> there are some battles to pick and there are some that are
> best to just, you know, try to go under the radar.

In this way, gender hedging continues to stand for some parents as a kind of protective strategy. The degree to which parents let this impulse to protect override their children's freedom surfaced as an enduring burden in their decisions and deliberations.

PARENTS' DISCURSIVE PRACTICES: THE LANGUAGE OF ACCEPTANCE, ADVOCACY, AND LOVE

Despite their earlier attempts to hedge around their child's gender nonconformity, parents increasingly give way to their child's preferences, per the child's persistence about how they wish to express themselves. Parents cross more and more boundaries between masculine and feminine and public and private, expanding the gendered horizons in which their children can express themselves— and in which they come to see gender normativity anew. As they do this, parents turn to the growing parent-advocate community for guidance and support, either via the internet or at support groups and conferences, and they seek to re-iterate its affirmative discourses within their own homes and families, engaging in a variety of different dialogues and conversations with their children. I describe this work as parents' *"discursive practices,"* a term I adopt from Winndance Twine's work on "racial literacy" described above, in which parents of biracial children engage their children in critical discussions about racism and push a progressive, anti-racist ideology within the family (92). These discursive practices are the major conduit through which parents teach and practice a more progressive gender ideology, both with their children and with others.

One of the major arms of parents' discursive practices is providing their children with an accessible language for talking about their gender-variant presentation with peers at school. Many parents testified to purposely offering their children these kinds of tools for when questions arise with other children. As Laurie said: "[M]ost of our talk about it has to do with response to social pressure ... we've had to develop a whole language around this. ... so he's always said he's a boy ... who likes girl things." Some parents honor the terminology that their children have derived themselves, such as "boygirl," "I'm both," or "I am just [Bo]."

Another critical facet of these discursive practices is parents advising their children about potentially less tolerant persons in society, and warning them about the questioning and stigma they might experience from those who "don't understand." Tellingly, Tracy analogized these kinds of lessons to the importance of talking about racism to children:

> I still think that we have to talk openly about what society is gonna expect because I think, just like with racism, you know, the research is really clear with racism that, you know, ignoring race and pretending it doesn't exist is not only white privileged behaviour but it's also really, it's not helpful to children, that they still are noticing it and that they are trying to make sense of society's racist views and they're still experiencing racism and they don't have a way to make sense of it.

Like many parents, Tracy will often dialogue with her child (gender-variant male, five years old) about the negative reactions he might get at school when he wears more feminine clothing, but she is sure to reiterate: "'[J]ust so you know, I don't think that's true [that it's weird for him to wear such things] ... do you wanna figure out what you might say to them?'" In these conversations, parents emphasize that though this prejudice is a reality their child will have to face, it is due to lack of awareness and understanding on other peoples' parts, and not anything related to the child.

Katy and Brian's approaches with their children exemplify these kinds of discursive practices. They constantly and consciously ask their child (gender-variant male, six years old) how he "feels on the inside," for "a window into gaining some insight" as to how he prefers to identify (i.e., as something more fluid or as a girl "all the way"), and seek to assure him that they will love and accept him no matter what. They also try to tap into how he feels about his body, and advise him that should he want it to look differently when he is older ("like Mommy's"), they can help make this happen with different "medicines." When reading books that feature boys and girls, they will take the opportunity to say, "Some boys have penises, and some boys have vaginas ... and that's okay." It is particularly interesting to note that the gender-normative siblings in these families are often included in these conversations. As a testament to the progressive ideological potential of this kind of parenting, Katy and Brian's gender-normative son once wore his brother's skirt to school, telling his friends that "boys can wear skirts, too."

Parents also try to promote a gender-inclusive dialogue outside of the home, either with their child's peers ("Didn't you know, pink is now a boys' colour too?" as one mother told an inquiring child) or with other parents. Many have sent letters to parents of the classroom that explain their child's gender variance and provide an accessible vocabulary for other adults and their children (templates of such letters are often shared among parents via support groups and internet mailing lists). Parents also negotiate with school administrations for staff training in gender variance, and help to re-write school policies to explicitly prohibit discrimination based on one's gender identity and expression. Evidently, in their transitions, parents begin to enunciate a more progressive ideology not only within their own families, but in their larger communities as well.

NEW BELIEFS ABOUT SEX AND GENDER

Over the course of their transitions, parents develop new understandings of sex and gender, cracking open previous belief systems that were grounded in the gender binary. Ally demonstrated this when she talked about consulting literature to "break apart [her] own gender schema" and embark on "this strange new territory." Ally represents many parents in this study whose previous ideology of gender has been radically uprooted in their journeys, supplanted by one that envisions a wider "spectrum" of gendered identities, expressions, and possibilities, regardless (but not always independent) of one's assigned birth sex. Ally reflected this kind of spectrum thinking when she mused about opening up another "space" for her child who did not quite identify as either a boy or a girl: "[I]f he could just have it exactly the way he likes, would he rather just have a whole 'nother space opened up for him that doesn't have to be just girl, just boy, and he just kind of *be*?" Similarly, Katy remarked that she preferred the idea of a "boy in a skirt" to sticking her child into the "girl box": "I liked this idea of going beyond the binary." Brian, her husband, also espouses a "spectrum":

> [T]he idea that you can have six billion people on the planet and have everyone neatly fit into one or two boxes, it's absurd ... how could you expect everyone to be either all this or all that?

A critical tenet of this re-conceptualization is parents' attempt to diminish the importance of genitals (or anatomical sex) from gender identity and development. As Shella put it:

> [I]t's amazing to watch somebody really be strong in who they are to try and tackle something huge, because okay, you're born with a penis, okay, you're a boy, boom, done— *no, not necessarily.*

CONCLUSION

Along with deconstructing the gender binary, parents also cited more awareness of and concern for LGBT issues, especially as these relate to gender-nonconformity (some have even started exploring the term "genderqueer" on behalf of their child). This is noteworthy, given that the majority of the parents in my sample are in heterosexual partnerships and are otherwise gender- and sexually-normative.[9] Prior to their "transition," many of the parents in my study rarely thought seriously about gender non-conformity (or conformity), transgender identity, and the gender binary. Indeed, Brian confessed that had he received a letter like the one he and Katy had sent out about their gender-variant child six years ago, he would have thought "something's not right" with the family. Now, however, parents think more critically about—and more readily observe around them—the strictures of gender to which we are conditioned and around which we organize so many behaviours. As a result, they feel personally connected to LGB and transgender issues, which have marked a deeply personal and tangible element in their daily lives. In many ways, they have become critical theorists of gender in their own right, and their experiences could point to major tectonic shifts in how more of the gender-normative "mainstream" thinks and talks about sex, gender, and sexuality. However "accidental" it may feel to them, these parents are blazing a new trail in societal acceptance of and advocacy for gender diversity, and are helping to build a safer and more inclusive world in which all children can learn and grow.

[1]Cisgender is used to designate *not* transgender.

[2]Of these sixteen children: eleven were assigned male at birth, five were assigned female at birth. None of the children were born with an intersex condition.

[3]See, for example, Carla Pfeffer's growing body of work on partners of trans men, including "Bodies in Relation--Bodies in Transition: Lesbian Partners of Trans Men and Body Image."

[4]See the chapter on "Coming Out Stories" in Devor's *FTM: Female-to-Male Transsexuals in Society* (421-46).

[5]Highly similar experiences are narrated in Maureen Reddy's memoir, *Crossing the Colour Line: Race, Parenting, and Culture.*

[6]There is a growing collective of trans youth advocacy organizations, web sites, and parent blogs, which articulate a particularly supportive discourse about childhood gender nonconformity and which parents can turn to for information and support.

[7]All names that appear in this piece are pseudonyms.

[8]Regarding terminology: in this piece, I honour the gender identities ("boy" or "girl") that children have claimed for themselves, such as the case of Theresa's child below, who was assigned "male" at birth, identifies exclusively as a "girl" and whom they now regard as their daughter (i.e., a "transgender girl"). For children who have not yet articulated firm gender identities ("boy"/"girl"/

something other), but who do not necessarily identify with the gender assigned of them (i.e., "boy"), I refer to their anatomical sex category designated at birth to signal their gender variance (i.e. "gender-variant male") and leave their gender identity unnamed and ambiguous, as in the case of Tim here. I use the pronouns the parents used at the time of our interviews.

[9]Among the parent-interviewees are represented: ten heterosexual partnerships; four same-sex/lesbian partnerships; and two single mothers whose children came from heterosexual partnerships.

WORKS CITED

Bryant, Karl. "In Defense of Gay Children? 'Progay' Homophobia and the Production of Homonormativity." *Sexualities* 11.4 (2008): 455-75. Print.

Devor, Holly [Aaron]. "Coming Out Stories." *FTM: Female-to-Male Transsexuals in Society*. Bloomington, IN: Indiana University Press, 1997. 421-446. Print.

Ehrensaft, Diane. *Gender Born, Gender Made: Raising Healthy Gender-Nonconforming Children*. New York: The Experiment, LLC, 2011. Print.

Green, Richard. *The "Sissy Boy Syndrome" and the Development of Homosexuality*. New Haven, CT: Yale University Press, 1987. Print.

Hope, Bedford. "REVIEW: Gender Born, Gender Made by Diane Ehrensaft, Ph.D." *Accepting Dad*. 17 June 2011. Web. 30 Oct. 2012.

Kane, Emily. *The Gender Trap: Parents and the Pitfalls of Raising Boys and Girls*. New York: NYU Press, 2012. Print.

Kane, Emily. "Policing Gender Boundaries: Parental Monitoring of Preschool Children's Gender Nonconformity." *Who's Watching?: Daily Practices of Surveillance Among Contemporary Families*. Eds. M. K. Nelson and A. I. Garey. Nashville, TN: Vanderbilt University Press, 2009. 239-259. Print.

Meadow, Tey. "'Deep Down Where the Music Plays': How Parents Account for Childhood Gender Variance." *Sexualities* 14.6 (2011): 725-747. Print.

Panitch, Melanie. *Disability, Mothers, and Organization: Accidental*

Activists. New York: Routledge, 2008. Print.

Pepper, Rachel. *Transitions of the Heart: Stories of Love, Struggle and Acceptance by Mothers of Transgender and Gender Variant Children*. Ed. Berkeley, CA: Cleis Press Inc., 2012. Print.

Pfeffer, Carla. "Bodies in Relation—Bodies in Transition: Lesbian Partners of Trans Men and Body Image." *Journal of Lesbian Studies* 12.4 (2008): 325-45. Print.

Reddy, Maureen T. *Crossing the Colour Line: Race, Parenting, and Culture*. New Brunswick, NJ: Rutgers University Press, 1994. Print.

Risman, Barbara J. and Kristen Myers. "As the Twig Is Bent: Children Reared in Feminist Households." *Qualitative Sociology* 20.2 (1997): 229–52. Print.

Thorne, Barrie. *Gender Play*. New Brunswick, NJ: Rutgers University Press, 1993. Print.

Twine, France Winddance. *A White Side of Black Britain: Interracial Intimacy and Racial Literacy*. Durham, SC: Duke University Press, 2010. Print.

13.
Our Fluid Family

Expression, Engagement and Feminism

LIAM EDGINTON-GREEN, BARRY EDGINTON AND FIONA JOY GREEN

W E'RE EXCITED BY THIS OPPORTUNITY to write about some of the ways in which our family has grown together to support one another in our unique personalities and identities. This chapter allows the three of us the occasion to recall and share our various remembrances of living as a fluid family over the past twenty-five years. We're consciously positioning this piece as a celebration of a childhood that has been successfully negotiated, despite the inevitable challenges and complications associated with not conforming to a narrow gender-binary. We are not overlooking the relatively few struggles we had, likely in part to the fact that we experienced a level of protection and privilege due to being white, members of the middle-class, and formally educated. Rather, we are focusing here on the joyous growth and valuable life experiences of our journey. One of the chief joys is the way we have developed a trusting and loving relationship that allows us to jointly write about our experience of gender fluid parenting practices. The chapter is divided into four sections where each family member—starting and ending with the youngest—introduces themself and speaks of their understanding and experiences of gender. Liam's voice bookends those of his parents, Barry and Fiona.

LIAM ~ EXPRESSION

In thinking about writing this paper and outlining what gender expression and gender fluidity means to me, I thought it would be helpful to start with an analogy. I am colourblind—a word laden with assumptions. Generally when I tell someone this, they assume that I cannot see colour at all. This often leads to two things: 1) People holding up different objects and asking what colour they are, and 2) Questions and confusion around how I can dress and coordinate my clothing so well—both humorous responses in their own right.

I then explain more specifically that I have red-green colour deficiency, which is understood as such: I can see colour just fine, the problem is that my brain doesn't understand where one colour stops and where another starts. It's the classification of colours by their names that I find difficult as the boundaries of each colour are fluid and meld into one another in my mind. This is a perfect parallel of how I saw gender as a child. I didn't see a skirt as female or a pair of overalls as male, I simply saw them as interesting. Now, having lived in a gendered and structured society for almost twenty-five years, I have learned where these boundaries exist; yet I still see them as fluid, in flux and open to my interpretation.

I feel that in not conforming to the gendered expectation placed upon me, I was able to directly see the mechanics of our society—the ways in which people think and act. I noticed patterns in thought and behaviour—if an adult thought that I was a girl, they would treat me in such a way, if they thought I was a boy, the way in which they interacted with me would be different. And lastly, if they thought I was a girl and then discovered I was a boy, a third type of interaction occurred.

I didn't like this last type of interaction as a child. It felt awkward and embarrassing both for me and the other individual. When someone reassessed my gender, I felt scrutinized, judged and completely vulnerable. It was as if they were not only redefining who I was in their mind in terms of gender, but also in terms of behaviour, intellect and ability. Questions then arose about my actions and behaviour, and that of my parents in allowing me to wear a patterned top, or wear my hair long. I'm sure, looking back on the situation with years of maturity, that some of these queries came from a place of intrigue and not judgment; however, at that age, any such question embarrassed me and made me feel different—not 'normal'. The easiest solution for me, then, was to entirely avoid these types of interactions.

If someone mistook me for a girl, I played along, and was happy to have a positive conversation with someone. I was not interested in making a statement, proving a point or educating someone on what gender meant to me. I simply wanted to explore my imagination, grow, live and surround myself with happiness and positivity. I saved myself and the other person from embarrassment, and went on my way. I never felt guilty in these instances. I guess then, I was happy enough knowing who I was, and did not need the approval of acquaintances and strangers.

In this way, I became a master of manipulation. I became so nimble at adapting to my situation that I felt no problems pretending to be a girl for a day—something that I distinctively remember doing around age 10 at a soccer camp. At this camp, kids were separated in the morning based on gender and age, and were put into small teams to practice and play against each other. However, during the break for lunch, all the kids were able to eat together and commingle. I remember making friends with a couple of girls that were at the camp. They mistook me for a girl and assumed that I was on a different team. I didn't know anyone else at this camp and was desperate to make friends—so I played along. I particularly remember the feeling of queasiness in my stomach, nervous that I would be found out, that I would pass into this third type of interaction, where others became aware that my gender did not align with their expectations. But, that never happened, lunch finished, and I went back to play with the other boys my age. I wasn't found out or scrutinized; in fact, no one took notice at all.

As I pointed out earlier, when adults interacted with me they changed their approach or their words based on my gender. If they thought I was a girl they would talk about my appearance, my pretty eyelashes or long hair; if I were a boy they would focus more on my actions and behaviour, commenting that I was well mannered, for instance. Yet, my experiences with kids my age demonstrated that they interacted with me on a human level and not on one simply based on gender. When perceived as female, the types of conversations we had were no different from those when perceived as male. Yet, when something came into contact with the conventions and social norms that shaped kids' lives—i.e. the realization that my gender was different than previously perceived—the interaction disintegrated, as the basis on which it was formed was suddenly questionable and not comprehensible. Then the resulting interaction paralleled the third type that occurred with adults.

The ability to think on my feet, adapt to situations and confidently back up my words with actions translated into other areas of my life. In high school I was involved in public speaking and debate. I did quite well, placing nationally throughout high school and making the national team and travelling to the World Individual Debating and Public Speaking Championships in my senior year. The categories that I was especially strong in were impromptu speech and impromptu debating, where I had to think on my feet with very little preparation to construct arguments to convince listeners of my position. In this way, I believe that the skills that I learnt as a child directly helped me in my adolescent years.

Attending private school for my elementary and senior years, where a uniform was required, meant that I didn't have much opportunity to express myself through fashion, nor to see other kids my age do the same. Throughout my adolescence, especially in middle school and my early high school years, I became conscious of my sexuality and gender expression. I wore typically male clothing and had short hair. I was not mistaken for a girl. Yet, it is important to note that I didn't feel pressure to stifle part of my creativity or part of who I was. My interests during that time simply changed and so did my expression of who I was.

It wasn't really until I came out as gay in my senior year and became involved in the queer community that I found others who expressed their gender in different ways. This intrigued me. I was introduced to a whole group of people and wanted to fit in, much like any teenager. I expressed myself more, started to wear some makeup, and introduced pieces of clothing normally found in the women's section of the store into my wardrobe. However, I didn't cross-dress or "dress up" as a woman. I simply liked the style of shirt found in the girl's section more than the boys and would wear it with jeans and sneakers. I found it silly that I was only supposed to shop in one section of the store and instead allowed myself to choose whatever I liked to fit my personal style. For example, when in high school (2004-2006), I would wear women's jeans as they fit me better than men's and I liked the skinnier pant. Men's jeans at that time were too baggy for my personal style and I found it hard to find a size small enough to fit my waist. Yet now, in 2013, the fashion has changed and I can easily find pants of this style in the men's department. I rarely shop in the women's section, not because my style has changed, but because there are different items at my disposal.

As a homosexual man involved in the queer community, I see a lot of different ways people express their gender. Just as with any large community, the queer community has factions, groups and divides. One of these divides is based on gender expression. While drag queens and kings are accepted as part of the queer community, they are often seen as novel, interesting and/or bizarre. Often they are fetishized by other members of the community and, from conversations that I have had with various queens, have a difficult time having serious relationships. People have a difficult time accepting and understanding their expression of gender, or are simply interested in them in a purely sexual way. So, it became quite a shock in the community when I dated a drag queen for more than two years. I never had any issue accepting my boyfriend's expression of gender, and understood that it was nothing to be feared. Just as he liked watching Japanese cartoons and eating Italian food, so too did he enjoy performance art and drag. I think that my own exploration with gender expression allowed me to feel comfortable with his and made me a more open and accepting person.

BARRY ~ ENGAGEMENT

It is difficult to talk of my approach to gender-fluid parenting without first speaking of my approach to parenting in general, and how I arrived here. My own history and family relations were not typical. I grew up in an immigrant family and was parented by my grandmother in my pre-school years. My mother's father owned a restaurant and most of my family worked there, including my mother. My father was non-existent and I only have one memory of meeting and talking with him. By the time I was ten-years-old, my mother was having difficulty caring for me and I was, for much of the time, left to grow up without a significant caregiver. In my early years I was put in the care of sitters and women who cared for me after school. My grandmother continued to care for me on weekends since my mother was working full time. Those who parented me were women and I had no father role model to follow. When I reached the fourth grade, I was becoming a problem and my mother made the decision to send me to a private, single-sexed, boarding school. Nuns were my teachers from Grades 4-8 and the Irish Christen Brothers ran my high school.

Regimentation, discipline and academics became the models from which I developed. Interestingly enough, gender was not an obvious issue. There were no girls whose behaviours were seen as different or alien. There was no: "don't act like a girl." Rather, the model was to behave as the person you are. In high school there were no gendered activities: for example, I was a cheerleader in grade 12. This may be an epiphenomenon of the time period (1950s and '60s), the particular school (Catholic Military), or the lack of an immediate relationship with a father who was trying to mold his son into the person he thought he should be. This last point encompasses not only father-son relations but also the gender relations within the family. Simply put, where else would I learn to act my gender or require others to act their specific gender in a world void of obvious gendered interactions: no family and no television. My experiential world was not governed by a rigid set of gender roles.

By the time I reached university, I had little or no experience with gender difference that would guide dating behaviour and general interactions with women in my university courses. At that time I also started reflecting on how I experienced other fathers and families. All this had an effect on my view of relationships, marriage and children. These experiences with women were strained since I never acted the way a 'typical male' was to act in a relationship. I had no model to follow. Thus, I gravitated to relations with women who were also not typical, i.e. those not seen as 'feminine.' It cannot be forgotten that this all happened in the 1960s, a time when many of the typical definitions of gendered roles were being challenged. Questions of self, image, and role within my relationships became a daily reminder that external displays of gender ceased to fit the model that defined clear boundaries of body image and social behaviour. I quickly learned that displays of self through body image became more than a statement of personal preference, displays of self became instances of social criticism: e.g. having long hair.

By the time I was in graduate school studying the social sciences, the groundwork for my ideas of gender display were established. I started to understand the issues of parenting, role-playing and gender display in a more theoretical and wider social context, as Mills writes in the *Sociological Imagination*. During my graduate years I was schooled in Marxist Humanism and Existential Psychology with a healthy dose of Critical Theory. This framework made me more critical of gender boundaries and I had no time for the bonds of marriage and the constraints of parenting work while studying the work of Michael Foucault.

These ideas held sway throughout my graduate studies and into my first years of teaching. During this time I met Fiona, who made me reflect upon my ideas of parenting, marriage and gender roles. I began to see that these role definitions and constraints could be challenged from the inside, and that the ideas of "feminist mothering" were not restricted to women.

All of the above may seem superficial but in my mind this personal self-history allowed me to become a parent. Since I had no experience with "fathering" my approach became based on the concept of "engagement," or becoming one with the relationship between parent and child in that moment. I liken this to Freud's idea that patients help themselves, and that the therapist is the conduit who allows this to happen. For me, then, the boundaries of self-expression are not pre-determined but emerge from the process of bringing all that I have learned to a specific moment. For example, when Liam was young he had very fine features, long eyelashes and liked to dress in very colourful clothing. Liam and I would go grocery shopping and at the check-out the cashier would ask my daughter's name. Liam replied "Liam"; this was usually translated into a girl's name like "Leanne" followed by the cashier saying that she was a beautiful girl. In these situations I withdrew from the interaction and did not correct the mistake. Liam simply smiled and said "Thank you." After, Liam and I would talk and try to understand why the cashier would mistake Liam's gender. These instances wouldn't trouble Liam or question his view of himself. However, this is a simple innocuous incident. On another occasion, Liam and I were in a bookstore and he wore a favorite dress. While Liam was reading on the floor I noticed that the principle of his school was at the front of the store. I thought that this might result in an embarrassing interaction for Liam. Instead of sheltering Liam from this incident I talked to him about the situation and we decided to leave the store from another door. By grade one I thought that Liam had a sense of himself and an understanding of how he would treat those seen as engaging in deviant behaviour.

Thus, I come to define the process of parenting that I practice as one of "engagement." I do not see this model to be specific to gender-fluid parenting but one that encompasses all parenting. In other words, the parent engages with the child to make possible the attainment of wants and needs which then become the basis for the development of self for both the parent and child. The guidance of the parent must always be there to assist the development of self. Bringing from their own prior experiences of knowledge, the parent must provide an environment of education, safety and self-realization. This may mean the "filtering" of specific ideas and influences, such as media, peers, schools and other adults. "Engagement" is for me the assistance of the parent in developing the self of the child and not the colonization of the persona of the child by a parent who wishes to live their idea of self through that of their child.

Part of the purpose of outlining my past and the development of my ideas is to show the principles that guide the process of 'engagement' and 'filtering.' When Liam was in pre-school he wanted to grow his hair long, and there was some pressure from friends, family and teachers to cut his hair so he would "look like a boy." In support for Liam's choice, I also grew my hair. Other incidents of "engagement" were my participation in activities. I was always amazed at how other parents would use their child's activities as a way to leave them to the care of others. My learning fantasy card games, attending soccer practices, and allowing Liam to dress as he wished are all instances of 'engagement.' You may ask, however, what happens when a child wants to engage in behaviour that may be dangerous. Like any parent who teaches their child about possible dangerous activity, many sports for example, we must bring to the situation our experience and a "sociological imagination."

Gender display plays a critical part in the development of self and attempts to limit the rigid definitions of how children should act or dress can become barriers to self-fulfillment. My parenting actions, as I feel would be the actions of many parents, are to prevent any possible embarrassment as larger social pressures and judgments invade the privacy of our family. I think that when parents engage their children in a process of self-development that respects the gendered choices and displays their children choose, the relationship between parent and child will enhance the lives of all of us.

FIONA ~ FEMINIST MOTHERING

From a young age, having internalized the hetero-normative narrative for white, middle-class, temporarily able-bodied, cisgendered, heterosexual girls, I assumed that I would birth and parent at least one child. With luck and relative ease, I conceived and birthed my son, Liam Seth Edginton-Green, twenty-five years ago. As I've written elsewhere, his birth profoundly changed me and brought my feminism to life in ways I never imagined (Green 2003, 2011).

My feminism is an integral part of my sense of self and all aspects of my life, including my parenting practice. It's also the basis of my respect for the autonomy of all humans, regardless of socially defined markers such as ability, education, ethnicity, gender, race, religion, sex, sexual orientation, and social class. In response to the demands placed on me by society and by my child to ensure his "preservation, growth and social acceptability," I've developed a maternal practice that includes what Sara Ruddick calls "maternal thinking" (Ruddick 1980, 1989). Through my particular practice of feminist mothering, I've always honoured my son's desire to express himself in ways that are true to him. Together with his father Barry, I willingly and consciously take on the responsibility of trying to create and protect a safe space where Liam can grow as, and develop into, himself.

I was acutely aware of this responsibility when Liam was a young child, particularly around his desire to explore his sense of identity through his keen attention to his own fashion and style. Reflecting back on those years, Barry and I were ahead of the current parenting practice of following the lead of one's children. We honored our son's exuberant and self-assured personality, as well as his clothing and activity choices when other parents were much less likely to do so. Unlike parents today, who, on the one hand, appear to be exposed to more child-rearing 'experts' and conflicting opinions than ever before, yet on the other, have access to multiple examples of child rearing that are shared by other parents through social media,[1] our parenting practices were seen by some to be odd, daring or on the margins of being dangerous.

When Liam was about two-and-a-half years old and asked me where his dress was, I intuitively responded with, "You don't have one. Would you like one?" My reaction to his quick reply of "Yes!" was to phone my sister to see if she had any dresses that my niece had outgrown and could give us. I delighted in Liam's carefree twirl the moment he put on his new pink crocheted dress from his older cousin. What else does one do in a flowing dress? While grocery shopping about six months later, Liam asked if I would buy him a pair of black patent leather Mary Jane 'party shoes,' just like the ones his girl friends wore for their birthday celebrations. I distinctly remember thinking, "Am I prepared to say, 'You have a penis; you can't wear party shoes?'" No. I refused to squash my child's spirit, expressed in his desire to dress himself this way, in order to defend and propagate patriarchal defined gender stereotypes. So Liam tried on the Mary Janes, did another one of his pleasure expressing pirouettes, and we bought and took home the new fancy shoes.

Liam's foray into wearing dresses, femme party shoes, decorating his room with bright floral wallpaper and vibrant paint, and wearing colourful hair wraps in his shoulder length hair was easy to support. It made him so very happy. Other folks in our small network also saw and enjoyed Liam's comfort and glee in his self-expression. His music teacher, along with the other children in his class and their parents, as well as his friends and care providers at his daycare simply accepted him as he was. Liam's ease with wearing socially defined girls clothes allowed other boys in his day care to more easily "dress up" outside the bounds of this often gender constrained playtime. Our personal friends enjoyed Liam's individualism and never questioned or negatively commented on his attire partly, I believe, because of our easy acceptance of and response to Liam. We never felt we had to explain Liam's choices to anyone; this is who Liam is and how he chooses to express himself. And we love and adore him for it.

There were others, however, who had difficulty with Liam's choices and our support of him. For instance, a local feminist suggested I was confusing Liam by allowing him to wear dresses and asked me if he knew he was a boy. Feminists at an academic conference accused me of 'de-masculinizing' him, and my mother questioned our wisdom in permitting what she called Liam's "cross-dressing" behaviour. Although we were never directly accused of forcing Liam to wear dresses, grow and wear his hair long, or decorate his bedroom like a middle-aged woman's, our parenting decisions and abilities were clearly being scrutinized and challenged.

Liam's entry into Kindergarten at a co-ed private school brought further inspection, particularly from other parents and older students who tried to figure out his gender. Most people did not recognize him as a boy; they often told me how beautiful my daughter was and directly asked me why she was wearing a boy's uniform. My response was to calmly agree that my son was beautiful and to note that he was not breaking the school dress code. Liam didn't appear to be bothered by people's discomfort and queries in and outside of school. For instance, when servers in restaurants mistook him for a girl, he and we didn't correct them; rather we'd enjoy our private little joke about their mistake or confusion.

As a family we talked about how boys and men don't generally wear dresses in Canada, and identified other cultures where it was more acceptable and normalized. Liam quickly learned who was supportive of his fashion choices and would decide what to wear in our home depending on who was coming over for a visit. He'd choose to wear long t-shirts with leggings, dresses or skirts when supportive friends shared their time with us and sweat pants or shorts when unsupportive folks visited. When we went for bike rides, Liam would often decide if he'd like to drop in on a friend or not after considering their attitude toward his particular outfit.

At times during his first few years in an all boys primary school, where all students wore the same uniform of button shirts, ties, pants, and short hair cut above the collar, others bullied Liam for not being über masculine. These personal attacks appear to be based on his fellow schoolmates believing that he was not appropriately expressing his male gender. Being highly intelligent, articulate, and quick-witted, Liam often handled these situations with cool sarcasm and mastered mockery. On the few occasions where we learned that physical altercations had taken place, Barry or I would speak with the administration and the situation was appropriately dealt with.

When he was about eight years old, Liam's sense of personal style shifted from dresses to brightly coloured tops and pants. A particular favorite was a leopard print velvety turtleneck with matching gloves. In the seventh grade, Liam found trustworthy friends in some of the girls who joined the school that year, and this new mixed-gender peer group of high performing students celebrated his uniqueness. The girls, in particular, had found a confidant and cherished equal in Liam.

Always aware of human diversity, in addition to gender fluidity, Barry and I spoke openly with Liam about the continuum of sexuality and the multiple and diverse ways in which people may decide to engage in sexually intimate relationships and create families. We had a number of middle-class gay and lesbian friends of various ages and ethnicities; some were in same-sex/gender relationships and others were single. Our community helped Liam understand from a very early age that people's choice of dress, gender expression, companions and relationships were various, flexible and not inherently tied to each other. Both our family and our community offered Liam space and multifarious examples of ways in which people express themselves and live their lives in relation to others. Sexuality, like gender, is fluid and open to exploration.

During the last year of high school, Liam began wearing subtle makeup on a daily basis and also dating a young man. His close friends at school were happy to see him in this new relationship and were cool with, and possibly even admired him for donning a pair of fairy wings during a non-uniform day celebrating Valentine's

Day. During the evening of his graduation celebration he turned the heads of many fellow students and parents as he walked proudly and confidently with his immaculately styled glam makeup and hair in his impeccably well fitted tailored suit and pink shirt that matched his date and best friend's dress. The following summer he participated, for the first time, in the Winnipeg Pride Parade that celebrates "a diverse community that supports or identifies with gay, lesbian, transsexual, transgender, intersex, two-spirit, and queer people" (Pride Winnipeg). Together with his former boyfriend, he chose to walk in the parade in full drag. In subsequent years he has chosen to wear a variety of clothes, from the relaxed summer attire of cut offs and t-shirts to dresses, wigs and high-heeled shoes, to march in the annual event.

As Liam approaches his mid-twenties, he continues to be keenly interested in fashion, stylized design, fine wine and gourmet cooking. While there are still moments of hostility and bullying from others, I'm confident that in doing our best to ensure that he had space while he was growing up to explore and express himself in ways that felt comfortable, he remains the self-assured, charming and charismatic person he's always been.

LIAM ~ FINAL WORDS

I'm so thankful to live in a world where I am accepted for who I am by my family, friends, co-workers, and in general, society at large—unfortunately many are not as privileged as me. There were moments of hardship and times where I felt uncomfortable and unsure—but having a respectful, supportive and open relationship with my parents meant that I was never alone or isolated. This support system has allowed me to feel comfortable with my own gender and expression and to see this as a source of power and strength. From my experience, being a confident and proud person and not apologizing for who you are is the most effective way to combat discrimination and homophobia. I am so happy to feel free of the confines of gender roles and expectations. I see how the system works, but have the knowledge to manipulate it to my gain. As Miranda Priestly, played by the genius Meryl Streep, says in *The Devil Wears Prada* when talking to her assistant/protégé,

"You can see beyond what people want and what they need and you can choose for yourself." How fantastic.

[1]For instance, there are a number of blogs that focus on raising gender non-conforming children, such as: *He Sparkles, Raising My Rainbow*; *George. Jessie. Love. Parenting and Loving a Transgender Kid*; *My Beautiful Little Boy*; and *Sarah Hoffman: On Parenting A Boy Who Is Different*.

WORKS CITED

Freud, Sigmund. *Five Lectures on Psycho-Analysis*. London: Penguin Press, 1995. Print.

George. Jessie. Love. Parenting and Loving a Transgender Kid. Web. Accessed January 3, 2013.

Green, Fiona J. "What's Love Got to Do With It? A Personal Reflection on the Role of Maternal Love in Feminist Teaching." *Journal of the Association for Research on Mothering*. 5 (2):47-56. 2003. Print.

Green, Fiona J. *Practicing Feminist Mothering*. Winnipeg: Arbieter Ring Publishing, 2011. Print.

HE SPARKLES Web. Accessed January 3, 2013.

Mills, C. Wright. *The Sociological Imagination*. Oxford: Oxford University Press. 2000. Print.

Pride Winnipeg. Web. Accessed January 3, 2013

Ruddick, Sara. Maternal Thinking. *Feminist Studies* 6 (2): 342-367. 1980. Print.

Ruddick, Sara. *Maternal Thinking: Towards a Politics of Peace*. Boston: Beacon Press. 1989. Print.

Raising My Rainbow. Web. Accessed January 3, 2013.

Sarah Hoffman: On Parenting A Boy Who Is Different. Web. Accessed January 3, 2013.

The Devil Wears Prada. Dir. Wendy Fincrman. Perf. Meryl Streep, Anne Hathaway, Stanley Tucci. 20th Century Fox Home Entertainment, 2006. DVD.

Contributor Notes

Arwen Brenneman started an arts degree, finished a science degree, and now works as a birth educator and doula. Her writing has appeared in *Herizons* and *Storyteller* magazines, as well as the upcoming collaborative novel *At the Edge*. She lives with her partner and their two boys in Vancouver, British Columbia.

Barry Edginton, Ph.D. is Professor and former Chair of the Department of Sociology at the University of Winnipeg. His research interest is in the relation between the built environment (hospital design) and treatment of the Mentally Ill. He has published and presented many papers on this topic.

Liam Edginton-Green holds a Bachelor of Arts (Honours) in French Linguistics from the University of Winnipeg. He enjoys cooking gourmet vegetarian food, reading both literature and crap fiction, philosophizing and playing soccer. When he grows up he'd like to be a spy and travel the world.

May Friedman blends social work, teaching, research, writing and parenting. May's passions include social justice and reality TV and she is firmly in favour of living with contradiction. She has published on the topics of motherhood and transnationalism and has recently presented on fat activism, mothers who are sex workers and social work pedagogy. May lives in downtown Toronto and plays with gender with her partner and three young children.

Fiona Joy Green, Ph.D. is a feminist mother who lives with her spouse of almost 30 years and their various pets. She teaches Women's and Gender Studies and currently holds the position of Associate Dean of Arts at the University of Winnipeg. Fiona has published on the subjects of feminist mothering, feminist maternal pedagogy, and on the depiction of mothers on reality TV. She's engaged in a collaborative research project exploring the ethics of mommy blogging and blogs for *Mommy Blog Lines: Tal(k) ing Care.*

Susan Goldberg is a writer, editor, essayist and blogger, and co-editor of the award-winning anthology *And Baby Makes More: Known Donors, Queer Parents, and Our Unexpected Families.* Her writing has been featured in *Ms.* magazine, *Lilith* magazine, and several anthologies. She blogs for VillageQ.com, *Today'sParent. com*, and at MamaNonGrata.com. Susan lives in Thunder Bay, Ontario, with her partner and their sons.

Jake Pyne is a community-based researcher and Ph.D. student in the McMaster School of Social Work. Jake has held a number of research and advocacy roles in Toronto's trans community over the past twelve years, most recently leading a series of initiatives focused on trans parents and gender independent children at Rainbow Health Ontario, the LGBTQ Parenting Network at the Sherboune Health Centre, Concordia University, the Re:searching for LGBTQ Health team at the Centre for Addiction and Mental Health, and the Centre for the Study of Gender, Social Inequities and Mental Health. Jake is a dad to two little ones in Toronto, who bowl him over with their wildness and love.

Elizabeth Rahilly is a Ph.D. Candidate and instructor in Sociology at UC Santa Barbara, with an emphasis in gender and sexuality. Her research concerns parents who raise and support gender-variant and transgender children. She previously received an MA in Sociology from UCSB and a BA in Anthropology from New York University. If you would like to hear more about Elizabeth's research with parents or are interested in contributing to her study, you can contact her at: erahilly.rc@gmail.com.

Damien W. Riggs is a senior lecturer in social work at Flinders University. He teaches in the areas of gender/sexuality, family studies, and critical race and whiteness studies, and is the author of over 100 publications in these fields, including *What About the Children! Masculinities, Sexualities, and Hegemony* (Cambridge Scholars Press, 2010). He is the editor of the *Gay and Lesbian Issues and Psychology Review.*

Sarah Sahagian is a Ph.D. candidate in gender, feminist and women's studies at York University in Toronto. Her writing has appeared in a variety of news and academic publications, including *The Journal of the Motherhood Initiative, The Beaverton* and *The Huffington Post.* Sarah is also the co-editor of the Demeter Press title *Mother of Invention: How Our Mothers Influenced Us as Feminist Academics and Activists.*

Sandra Schneider is an Assistant Professor of Education in the School of Teacher Education and Leadership, Radford University. Her research interests include: class, race and gender in education and educational reform activism. Sandra's latest area of research explores homeschooling and unschooling parenting practices and mothering identities.

Jessica Ann Vooris is a Ph.D. graduate student and undergraduate instructor in Women's Studies at the University of Maryland, College Park. She received her BA in Women's Studies and Creative Writing at Bucknell University in 2009. Her research addresses questions around LGBTQ parenting and family, the concept of the queer child, and parenting gender-creative children. She is a dual-citizen of the United States and Great Britain.

j wallace believes that each one of us gets to be the absolute experts on our own lives, and is particularly interested in creating more room and possibilities around sex, sexual orientation and gender identity. j is an Equity Program Advisor with the Toronto District School Board's Gender-Based Violence Prevention Unit, and an educator, an activist, a trainer and a writer. j is completing a Masters of Education at OISE/UT celebrating ways to create schools and classrooms that celebrate all gender identities. j also works with The LGBTQ Parenting Network in Toronto, developing and facilitating both *Transmasculine People Considering Pregnancy*, and *Queer and Trans Family Plannings*. j's family includes a two children, a husband, and an eclectic and fabulous constellation of chosen family. j's professional website is www.juxtaposeconsulting. com, and he blogs at www.http://ishai-wallace.livejournal.com/ often about the intersections of gender, education and parenting.

Jane Ward is associate professor of Women's Studies at the University of California Riverside. She is the author of *Respectably Queer* (2008), as well as several articles on queer politics, transgender relationships, heteroflexibility, the failure of diversity programs, and, most recently, queer motherhood. She teaches courses in feminist and queer studies, and is also an amateur parent, an angry low-femme, and a baker of pies.

Kathy Witterick is a violence prevention educator, La Leche League Leader and small business owner. She parents with David Stocker in Toronto, Canada and is honoured to be unschooling her three children: Jazz (seven), Kio (four) and Storm (two).